ELECTRIC VEHICLE TECHNOLOGIES

DAVID J. BRICKNELL

David J Bricknell

Copyright

Acknowledgements

I should like to thank the various EV groups, covering many different vehicles, for the inspiration for this book. This book covers the technologies that apply across all Electric Vehicles.

There are a number of laboratories and government testing organisations that have published a great deal on Electric Vehicles that is now in the public domain. These include:

- Argonne National Laboratory (anl.gov) [1]

- Idaho National Laboratory Advanced Vehicle Testing (avt.inl.gov) [2]

- Environmental Protection Agency (epa.gov)[3]

- HORIBA MIRA Ltd (formerly the Motor Industry Research Association) (horiba-mira.com)[4]

- National Renewable Energy Laboratory NREL (nrel.gov) [5]

- Oak Ridge National Laboratory (ornl.gov) [6]

- The Battery University [7]

Cover picture courtesy of By Andrzej Otrębski - Own work, CC BY-SA 4.0

Preface

In 2016, after buying my first Electric Vehicle and realising that there were many things to know about how they worked, I wrote my first book on EVs specifically addressing the BMW i3. I was delighted by the reception the book received and went on the write books on the Jaguar I-Pace and Tesla Models 3 and Y.

In 2020 there are now so many EVs available, more than I can write about, but the underlying technologies are similar across them all. This book addresses the technologies that EVs use rather than delve into the details of each particular model.

April 2020

David J. Bricknell CEng FRINA BSc (Hons)

Other EV books by David Bricknell

- **Electric Vehicles and the BMW i3** [8] [9]

- **Joining the Electric Vehicle Revolution: the things you need to know about how your EV works** [10]

- **Electric Vehicles and the Jaguar I-Pace** [11]

- **Electric Vehicles and the Tesla Model 3** [12]

- **Electric Vehicles and the Tesla Models 3 and Y** [13]

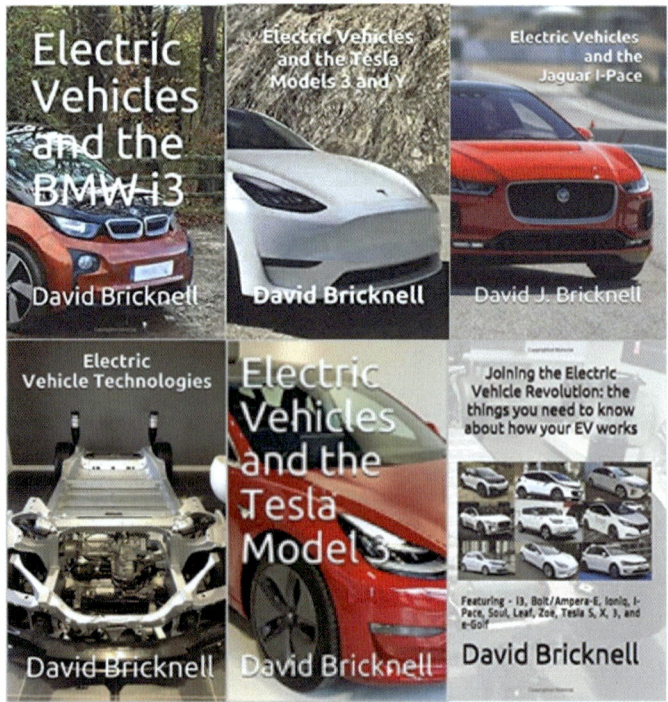

REVIEWS

Reviews of "Electric Vehicles and the BMW i3"

Jonathan Musk – Editor Autovolt Magazine

If you're after a more technical understanding of electric cars, this brilliant ebook by David Bricknell is a fascinating in-depth look at the inner workings of an electrified car. The author's impressive engineering background in shipbuilding and hybridisation shows, but the book has far wider appeal. The book attempts to describe the fundamentals of what makes an EV and attempts to make a hugely complex topic accessible to a wide audience. It makes for compulsive tech-geek reading and is thoroughly recommended no matter whether you already own an EV, want one or are interested in how they work.

Autovolt Magazine July / Aug 2016 www.autovolt-magazine.com

John Murray - Author of Supercharged Momentum [14]

This book is a great read for any EV owner not just for us i3 folk. I have learnt even more about my car through this book. David Bricknell goes into the technical details more than most. His scientific style uses numerous diagrams and graphs, along with clear explanations about the many intricacies of electric cars making concepts that are new to most motoring enthusiasts, clearly understandable. While centred on the brilliant BMW i3, there are lots of references to, and explanations about, others EVs as well making this book important for anyone considering the purchase of an electric car. Particularly relevant, comprehensive and well explained are the sections on that core aspect of electric cars, the battery. Issues of capacity, chemistry, longevity, temperature, charging and management are now even better understood, yet I have been driving an i3 for 18 months. Thanks to David for his work on this text.

Tom Moloughney – Charging Ahead Consulting
https://bmwi3.blogspot.com

The book is filled with information about the i3 that isn't available anywhere else. You don't have to be an i3 owner to appreciate the amount of technical details that David has put together here. I definitely recommend getting a copy if you're interested in electric cars.

I'm two weeks out from delivery of a 2018 i3S ReX and after spending 100+ hrs reading every EV forum imaginable trying to get EV literate, this book added on to the necessary engineering bits about the BMWi3. If you are somewhat of an EV nerd and need to know everything about this car, you have found a good book! It will help quantify the 'it depends' answers to range, charging speed, temperature effects, etc., while comparing the way BMW does things to Tesla, Nissan, Kia, etc. Cool knowledge to have and share with all of the EV onlookers. - A. Berger

———————

Having recently purchased an I3 ReX, I sat down and read the whole book in one sitting. I'm sure I'll be back for more in-depth study in the future. It's a very well-written and well-researched book! – J Francis

———————

Everybody owning or thinking of buying a BMW i3 should read this well written book.
I learnt a lot about the electric vehicle I will soon get.
And the book also made me become more interested in the technical side of battery electric vehicles in - Tor Helge Lyngstøl

———————

Reviews of "Joining the Electric Vehicle Revolution: the things you need to know about how your EV works":

The best book I've found so far about Electric Vehicles and the different types of batteries, chargers, and how it affects range and ease of use. The book is very recent (end of 2018) and really presents the technology as it is today. It's moderately technical (need to understand the basic concepts of electricity like voltage and amperage) and will please anybody who wants to go deeper than the surface and understand where the difference of performance between a Nissan Leaf and a Tesla is coming from.

Jonathan Musk – Editor Autovolt Magazine

As a long-time owner of a BMW i3, Bricknell has delved into the inner workings of electric vehicles over a number of years. His latest book expands knowledge to the most popular examples of electric vehicles on the new and used market today, as well as exploring forthcoming important models like Jaguar I-Pace. The book is more technical than most, which should satisfy anyone interested in the differences between the various electric powertrain approaches, including their dynamics, battery, charging, motors and inverters, and cooling and heating. In essence, the book is ideal for learning how EVs actually work, whether that's for owners wishing to know more about the gubbins beneath the bonnet or for those interested in the renaissance of electric power for automobiles.

Autovolt Magazine July - October 2018 www.autovolt-magazine.com

Reviews of Electric Vehicles and the Jaguar I-Pace

Highly recommended, good detail and very interesting throughout.

Reviews of Electric Vehicles and the Tesla Model 3

The book really is worth a look, particularly if you enjoy learning about the technical side of how the Model 3 works.
James Moore – Moderator Tesla Model 3 UK

A must have accessory for your EV!
This book is a great read. Whether you are new to EVs and are looking for an overview of how things work or you already have an EV and want to know the detail this book delivers nicely.

You will find a well-organized index and not only will it answer your questions, but will fill in information around the subject

Book you must read if you want more understanding of the M3 - Wilco
the second book written similar to the one about BMWi3. gives a good understanding about the tesla model 3. when you want to know more about the battery, system electronics and heating, performance, driving and charging, read this book. very informative.

LEAVE US A REVIEW

I hope you enjoy this book. If you do, **please leave a review** on Amazon. It will be a great help to future readers.

Abbreviations

A	Amps
AC	Alternating Current
A/C	Air Conditioning
APRF	Advanced Powertrain Research Facility - Argonne Laboratories
Ah	Amp Hours
ANL	Argonne National Laboratory
apu	Auxiliary Power Unit
AVT-INL	Advanced Vehicle Testing - Idaho National laboratory
AWD	All-Wheel Drive
BEV	Battery Electric Vehicle
BEVx	BEV Extended range
BMS	Battery Management System
C	Celsius (also sometimes called Centigrade)
CARB	California Air Resources Board
CEV	Combustion Engine Vehicle
CHAdeMO	CHArge de MOve
C-rate	Charge/discharge rate
CC	Constant Current
CCS	Combined Charging System
CdA	Drag Coefficient x Frontal Area
CFC	ChloroFluoroCarbon
CH_4	Methane
CO_2	Carbon Dioxide
COPD	Chronic Obstructive Pulmonary Disease
CSSU	Cell Supervision Sensor Unit
CV	Constant Voltage
DC	Direct Current
DOD	Depth of Discharge
DSC	Dynamic Stability Control
EGR	Exhaust Gas Recirculation
EIExSM	Electrically Excited Synchronous Machine
EME	Electrical Machine Electronics
EPA	Environmental Protection Agency
EV	Electric Vehicle
EVSE	Electric Vehicle Supply Equipment
F	Fahrenheit
GDI	Gas Direct Injection
GHG	Green House Gases
GWP	Global Warming Potential
HEV	Hybrid Electric Vehicle
HFC	HydroFlouroCarbons
hp	horse power
HSM	Hybrid Synchronous Machine
HV	High Voltage
ICE	Internal Combustion Engine
ICEV	Internal Combustion Engine Vehicle
IEC	International Electrotechnical Commission
IGBT	Insulated-Gate Bipolar Transistors
IM	Induction Motor
IP	Intellectual Property
IPM	Interior Permanent Magnet Motor
Kg	kilo gram
kph	kilometres per hour
km/h	kilometres per hour

Electric Vehicle Technologies

kW	kiloWatt
kWh	kiloWatt hour
LCO	Lithium Cobalt Oxide
LFP	Lithium Iron (Ferrous) Phosphate
LIB	Lithium Ion Battery
LMO	Lithium Manganese Oxide
LNO	Lithium Nickel Oxide
LRU	Lowest Replaceable Unit
LTO	Lithium Titanate Oxide
LV	Low Voltage
MCR	Maximum Continuous Rating
MIRA	Motor Industry Research Association
MOSFET	Metal Oxide Semiconductor Field-Effect Transistor
Mph	miles per hour
N&V	Noise and Vibration
NCA	Nickel Cobalt Aluminium
NEDC	New European Driving Cycle
Nm	Newton metre
NiCd	Nickel Cadmium
NiFe	Nickel Iron
MNiMH	Nickel Metal Hydride
NMC	Nickel Manganese Cobalt
NMH	Nickel-Metal Hydride
NREL	National Renewable Energy Laboratory
NO	Nitrous Oxide
NOx	Nitrogen Oxides – normally Nitrogen Dioxides
PHEV	Plug-in Hybrid Electric Vehicle
PM	Particulate Matter
PMSM	Permanent Magnet Synchronous Machine
PMSRM	Permanent Magnet Synchronous Reluctance Machine
PMSyRM	Permanent Magnet Synchronous Machine
PWM	Pulse Width Modulation
ReX	Range eXtender
rpm	revolution per minute
RFID	Radio Frequency Identification
SEI	Solid Electrolyte Interphase
SCR	Selective Catalytic Reduction
SI	System International
SiC	Silicon Carbide
SOC	State of Charge
SOx	Sulphur Oxides normally Sulphur Dioxide
SOH	State of Health
SRM	Switched Reluctance Motor
SRPMM	Switched Reluctance Permanent Magnet Machine
SUV	Sports Utility Vehicle
THD	Total Harmonic Distortion
UDDS	Urban Dynamometer Driving Schedule
V	Volts
Wh	Watt hours
WLTP	**W**orldwide harmonised **L**ight vehicle **T**est **P**rocedure
WRSM	Wound Rotor Synchronous Machine
ZEV	Zero Emissions Vehicle

Table of Contents

Electric Vehicle Technologies

This page left intentionally blank

Introduction

In broad terms there have been **Four Ages of Electric Vehicles**. The first three coming about due to a mixture of social, environmental, financial, regulatory or technological reasons but which ultimately failed either because the technology couldn't match the performance and costs of the Internal Combustion Engine ICE or the regulations were insufficiently demanding to force the change. This book looks in detail at the key technologies and regulations that will ensure that this age, the fourth, will be here for some time to come.

For those that have driven a BEV, it becomes immediately obvious that the **dynamics** are different: the instant torque giving smooth and immediately available acceleration and energy regeneration providing simple one-pedal driving. A Combustion Engine Vehicle (CEV) provides a different driving dynamic and these are contrasted graphically with those from a BEV.

The **battery** is of course the key to mobile electric transportation and today's battery developments are core to the recent rapid uptake of EVs. The historical battery types and the technological reasons for the current dominance of the Lithium Ion Battery LIB are discussed together with the various electrode chemistries and competing cell formats. Battery performance and life, a whole new area for most BEV drivers, are discussed and near/medium term future developments are also addressed.

A battery is an accumulator and stores energy generated elsewhere. Once depleted, **recharging** is necessary. For most drivers, their BEVs will be recharged at home, often whilst they are sleeping. On-route charging infrastructure is still growing rapidly both in number and in charging power – rapid chargers are now delivering 250kW and units are being installed capable of 350kW (useful once battery packs are able to take this level of power).

Energy stored in the battery is delivered through **power electronics** to the **motor**. Power Electronics have been key to maximizing energy efficiency through efficient control of the motor. Recently, the IGBT (Insulated-Gate Bipolar Transistors) has begun to be displaced by the more efficient and capable SiC-MOSFET (Silicon Carbide Metal Oxide Semiconductor Field-Effect Transistor).

Manufacturers are currently adopting different **motor technologies** to address the competing pressures of costs, size, efficiency and environmental friendliness; a few manufacturers are using third parties for this technology but most are now investing in their own developments and their own Intellectual Property IP – small size, high efficiency and low cost are key requirements for successful mass market BEVs.

It often comes as a surprise to BEV drivers that their electric car has a radiator. **Cooling of key drivetrain components,** particularly battery, motor and power-electronics, is the key to sustaining high performance.

Whilst cabin cooling through air-conditioning is much the same as combustion engine cars, **heating** is quite different as there is no waste heat from the combustion engine inefficiencies. For those BEVs with relatively small battery packs, heating can be a significant drain in deepest winter, many manufacturers are including heat pumps, to reduce the impact of lower temperatures.

The **environment** and the increasingly tighter **regulations** surrounding transport is one of the reasons for the latest growth of BEVs. Both Green House Gases GHGs and 'toxic pollution' are addressed and are often in opposition – one of the key mistakes behind the push for increased diesel adoption was the rush for lower CO_2 at the expense of increased NOx and PMs.

Wherever possible the charts included in this book are multi-axes in order to avoid repetitively showing the same information each using System International SI, Imperial, and the UK's hybrid of SI-Imperial. Whilst the charts are a little busier to read, this is considered preferable three versions of each chart – please check the axes when studying

This page left intentionally blank

Four Ages of Electric Vehicles

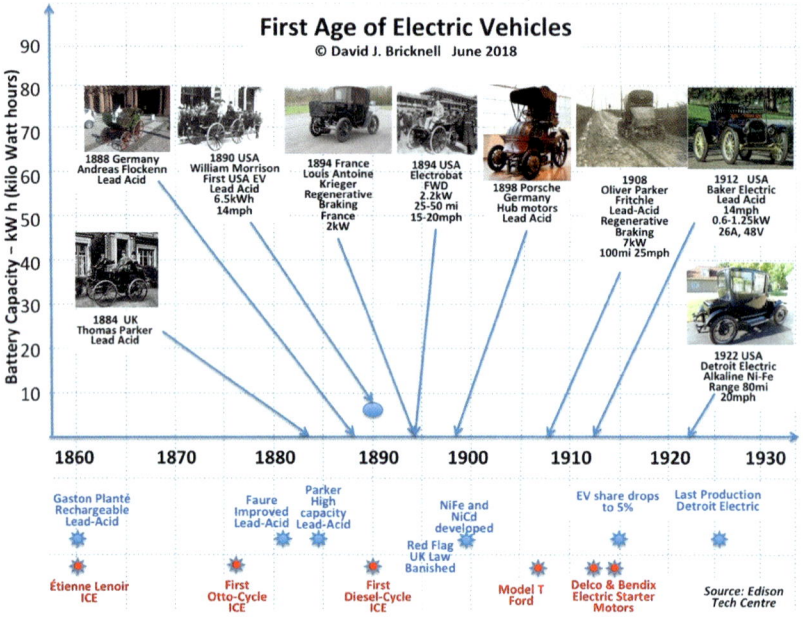

What could be described as the first age of Electric Vehicles was also the first age of motor vehicles. Coach built horseless carriages in appearance, these vehicles used lead-acid batteries and simple rheostat controlled electric motors for maximum speeds of about 20mph. Range, given the slow speeds and limited accelerations, was around 50-100 miles. Recharging took a very long time and electricity wasn't always easily available in all homes.

Ultimately competition from Combustion Engine Vehicles proved too great even though they were considerably more challenging to drive. Higher speeds, quicker refuelling and greater range coupled with significantly lower price from vehicles such as the Model T eventually won the day

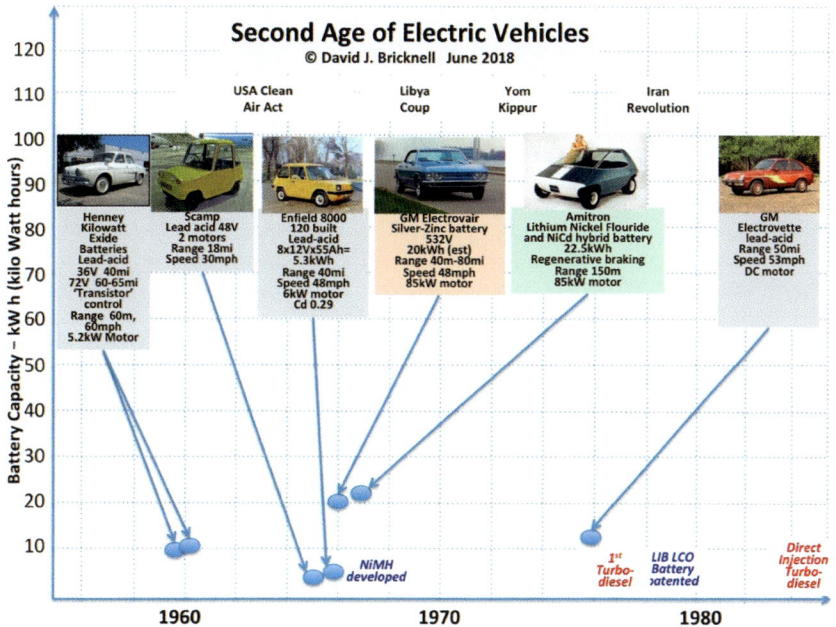

Second Age of Electric Vehicles
© David J. Bricknell June 2018

By the 1960s, pressure for cleaner air led to renewed interest in electric cars and by the 1970s severe oil price shocks resulting from the Libya coup, Yom Kippur war and the Iranian revolution further encouraged these developments, but a credible competitive car was not still not possible.

Lead Acid batteries still dominated energy storage but Nickel Metal Hydride NiMH, Silver-Zinc, and a Lithium Nickel Flouride/ Nickel Cadmium NiCd hybrid, were all tried.

Transistor control of motors improved efficiency and driveability.

The now ubiquitous consumer-electronics LCO Lithium Ion battery was patented in this period.

Meanwhile CEV vehicles saw the introduction of the highly efficient direct injection, turbodiesel.

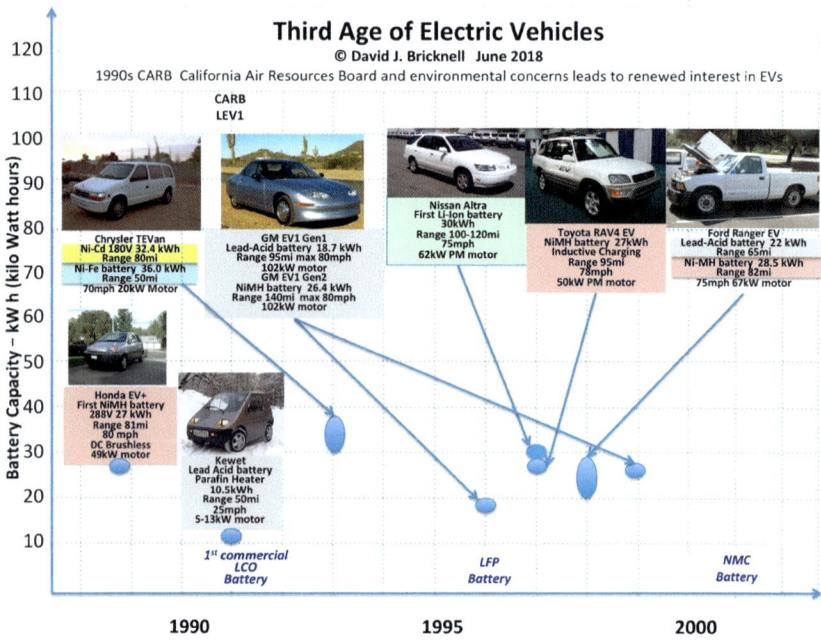

Third Age of Electric Vehicles
© David J. Bricknell June 2018
1990s CARB California Air Resources Board and environmental concerns leads to renewed interest in EVs

By the 1990s, renewed pressure for clean air led to the California Air Resources Board drive to improve vehicle efficiency and reduce emissions.

This led to a number of BEVs including the much-loved GM EV1.

Most significant though was probably the Nissan Altra with the first use of a Lithium Ion battery!

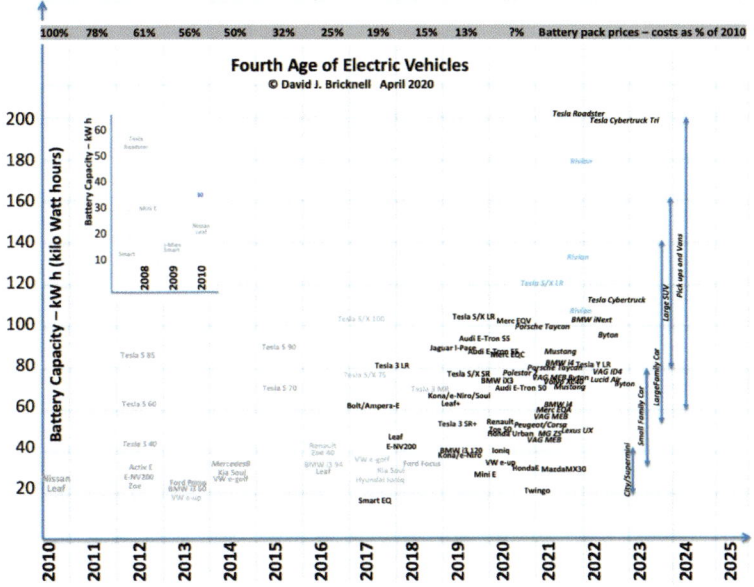

The fourth age, the one we are in now, began on two fronts. Tesla produced the Roadster offering serious range for the first time coupled with strong performance. [15] Tesla's strategy was to follow this with a large BEV and then a bigger selling mid-size BEV strategy. Across the Atlantic came the smaller Nissan Leaf offering, a more modest range and performance.

Tesla continued to produce longer and longer-range premium cars whilst other manufacturers dipped their toes tentatively into this new technology often with very little enthusiasm whilst still trying to fund ever more demanding regulations for combustion.

In the mean-time battery pack prices dropped in 2020 to 7% (not from) of that in 2010. [16]

By 2017, the direction of travel of future cars was clear and most manufacturers looked much more seriously at BEVs, some with extreme reluctance and the occasional rear-guard action. By 2020, the key issue against widespread sales of BEVs are sufficient battery supplies, shortfall in charging infrastructure and a motor industry focussed and configured around selling and repairing combustion engines – another Kodak moment!

This page left intentionally blank

Dynamics and Performance

Overview

The power and the energy required to drive a vehicle over a route are the same whether it comes from a tank of fossil fuel and a combustion engine or from a battery and electric motor – the differences are in the technology that translates the stored energy into power and motion.

Electric motors make BEVs both easy and fun to drive; they have rapid and responsive acceleration, one-pedal driving, no clutch and only one fixed gear. BEVs are catching combustion cars on range and are improving on recharging times – battery technology is rapidly developing.

Both speed and acceleration, delivered by motors, are directly related to battery capacity. Keeping the battery discharge rate, the rate at which you extract energy from the battery, low in order to prolong battery life is important along with keeping the motor and motor drive (inverter) within their temperature limits. Both of these issues are key to higher performance and to higher continuous speeds - significant improvements have been made in recent times to both these issues.

Range is a product of the battery stored energy against the energy used for accelerating and for sustaining speed. Battery capacity though isn't an absolute value - it varies with cell temperature, with rate of charge and discharge, with calendar time and with the number of charge/discharge cycles. Range also varies with vehicle speed in exactly the same way as it does in a combustion vehicle – the faster you go, or the more aggressively you drive, the quicker the energy store is depleted.

Cabin cooling is well understood with CEVs but for a BEV the amount of energy required for cabin heating in colder climes can be considerable. Cabin heating of an CEV is essentially done using (free) waste heat whereas the BEV has to generate it from the same battery energy that also provides range. Heat pumps can significantly improve the situation at the expense of complexity.

BEVs are zero-emissions at the point of use - emissions are not often considered to be a performance-criteria but for today's combustion engines it is the technical area that is demanding most investment. BEV emissions are related to the electrical generation source: in most countries power station emissions are lower per kWh than those produced by CEV and lead to significantly lower emissions per mile or kilometre. [17]

Battery capacity of cars is increasing quickly – For Tesla, from 40kWh to 100kWh (2020); for other manufacturers 20kWhrs (-2016) giving way to 30kWhrs (2016-2018) and 40-100kWhrs (2018-).

The most significant issue affecting widespread BEV adoption is the highway/motorway charging infrastructure: larger capacity battery packs and higher-powered on-route chargers (100, 250, and 350kW).

Key Components

Electric Vehicles all use essentially the same key components albeit they use different variants of each component type. Early 'fourth age' BEVs used readily available and generally off-the-shelf components and integrated them into the vehicle. Many manufacturers chose to develop their own critical components and BEV specific technologies, registering their own Intellectual Property in order to build value and to gain the advantage in the market, whilst others turned to specialist component companies to provide key electrical components such as batteries, motors and drives. It's maybe too early to know which is the right business model: for CEV, owning the engine and its technology was a core capability and one suspects that battery, motor or drives will be the new 'core'.

BEVs use the following key components:

A **High-Voltage HV battery** - in automotive terms, high-voltage means typically 300V-450V although 800V and above has appeared now in some EVs[18]. HV batteries are today always variants of Lithium Ion using different configurations (cylinder/prismatic or pouch), different chemistries (NCA, LMO, NMC or LFP electrodes and liquid or polymer electrolytes), and different configurations (serial or serial/parallel, depending on the cell capacity and power required). Voltages beyond 1kV are quite likely for future heavy goods vehicles just as they are currently in larger marine applications.

A **Low Voltage LV battery**, usually 12V, is used for initialising the HV system, for powering the systems used for accessing the car, and for systems such as the alarm system and entertainment. The LV battery is charged from the HV battery via a DC-DC link. Whether 48V systems will be in place of 12V, now that 48V is becoming more commonplace, or eventually become incorporated within the HV system, is yet to be seen.

A **motor or motors** usually either an Asynchronous (Induction) Machine, Synchronous Machines, or Switched Reluctance Machines. Motors can be arranged to drive the front wheels, the rear wheels, both front and rear wheels and even all four independently. Permanent magnet motors use either ferrous or rare-earth permanent magnets. Wound Synchronous and Induction Motors do not use rare earth magnets. Highly controllable power electronics, IGBTs and now SiC-MOSFET, has enabled reluctance motors to be used providing the highest levels of efficiency.

Road capable BEVs all use a **single-speed fixed gear** - motors have sufficient torque and rpm range to enable the use of a single-speed gearbox giving a credible top-speed with good acceleration and uninterrupted energy regeneration. Full torque at zero-speed eliminates the need for a clutch.

A **drive or inverter/rectifier** is used to convert battery DC to 3-phase AC (and back again during regeneration), and for controlling vehicle speed. Today's Inverters utilise power electronics (IGBTs and SiC-MOSFET) either in a six-pack or multiple six-packs depending upon the total power required: each pair addressing one of the phases and each one within the pair addressing the positive or negative part of the AC wave. Each motor will have its own dedicated inverter drive.

A **cooling system** is necessary for the electronic and electrical components, usually involving a water-glycol mix circulating through the components and then shedding heat through a front mounted radiator/fan combination.

A **battery cooling system** for use during hard driving, long journeys or when charging at elevated temperatures. This system can be forced air, water-glycol or a refrigerant system. Few BEV manufacturers retain passive thermal management.

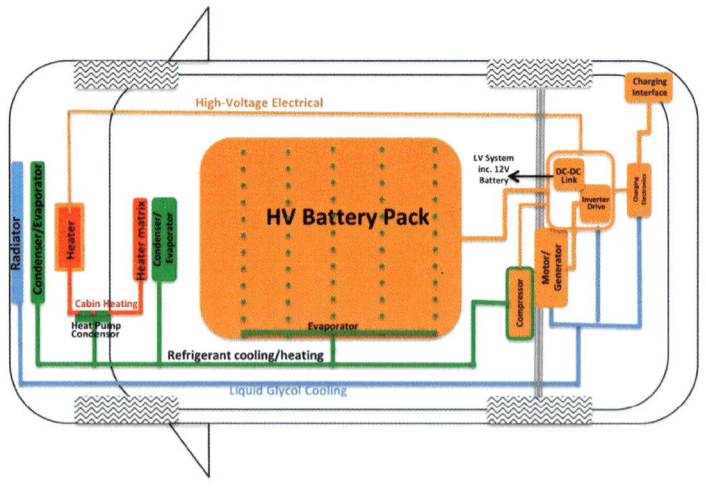

Key-Components schematic showing the HV electrical components and cooling systems. This shows a rear drive vehicle with battery cooling from refrigerant circuit whilst others use either water-glycol, forced or natural air-cooling of the battery and sometimes no cooling except passive heat transfer. Some BEVs are front-wheel drive, some are rear wheel drive, and some are all-wheel drive. Arguably, the BEV heating and cooling system is becoming the most complex system in the car.

A few BEVs use a Range eXtender, either of an ICE type or a fuel cell. For the ICE range-extender, a reciprocating or rotary combustion unit, fuel tank, injection and exhaust treatment are necessary but also an alternator, an inverter (AC to DC) and its own cooling system will also be included.

Overall Vehicle Efficiency

As with any propulsion system, losses are incurred at every energy conversion. Battery Electric Vehicles (BEVs) are very efficient at converting grid-derived electricity into vehicle motion.

There are inefficiencies or losses in the national distribution grid, the charging rectifier, the round trip to and from the battery, the motor drive inverter, the motor, and the gear and final drive.

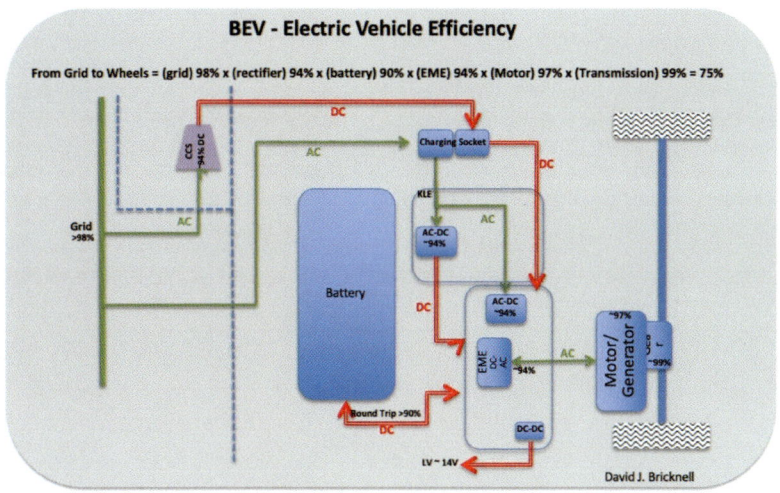

Typical efficiency of a Battery Electric Vehicle

Resistance and Power

At a steady speed (on level ground and with no wind) there are two principal components of vehicle resistance: rolling resistance and aerodynamic resistance - additionally, accelerating the vehicle will also require energy to overcome kinetic resistance.

Wind and hills will also affect vehicle aerodynamic resistance either up or down.

Vehicle weight is the key factor for rolling resistance whereas the vehicle's frontal area and its drag coefficient are the key factors for aerodynamic resistance.

Aerodynamics resistance dominates at higher vehicle speeds whereas rolling resistance dominates at lower speeds.

Rolling Resistance accounts for the energy required to overcome the resistance offered by the tyre during rotation. All vehicles, BEVs as well as CEVs, drive through wheels and pneumatic tyres.

Energy loss is due to the deflection of the tyre sidewalls and to the deflection of the tread blocks – new tyres present greater energy loss than worn tyres due to the deeper tread blocks. Tyres also scrub and slip, dissipating energy as they do so.

As a good approximation the force required to overcome rolling resistance is proportional to the weight of the vehicle and the coefficient of rolling resistance; the greater the vehicle weight and the higher the tyre's rolling coefficient the higher the resistance and the more power that is required. For a vehicle's pneumatic tyre, the coefficient of rolling resistance will increase a little as the vehicle's speed increases but this increase is small in comparison to the increase in aerodynamic resistance at higher speeds.

Resistance will increase when going uphill in response to the car's weight and relative to the steepness of the hill, and equally it will decrease when going downhill.

Whilst larger diameter tyres will reduce rolling resistance - two-inch in diameter increase bring a reduction of around 5% in rolling resistance[19]. Wider tyres increase rubber contact area and increase air resistance.

Performance tyres often have less energy efficient tread patterns, are generally lower profile, and are wider and mounted on larger heavier un-aerodynamic wheels. An increase in resistance is normally seen with these configurations.

Both rain and ambient temperatures will also affect rolling resistance through colder tyres and added surface water and rain drop resistance. [20]

Aerodynamic Resistance accounts for the energy required to propel the vehicle through the air. Resistance is proportional to the square of the vehicle speed and power is proportional to the cube of the speed.

Air density changes will affect resistance, offering higher aerodynamic resistance at colder temperatures due to denser air.

Wind speed will either increase aerodynamic resistance (head winds) or decrease aerodynamic resistance (tail winds) thereby either increasing or decreasing the power required to maintain a speed.

Reducing the frontal area of the vehicle to improve the aerodynamics will normally lead to an increase in vehicle length if internal volume is to be maintained and increasing vehicle length will increase weight and so a balance has to be sought between lowering rolling resistance and lowering aerodynamic drag.

The cross-over point between rolling resistance and aerodynamic resistance will vary between vehicles depending on the relative weights and aerodynamics.

Total Resistance is the sum of Rolling Resistance and Aerodynamic Resistance.

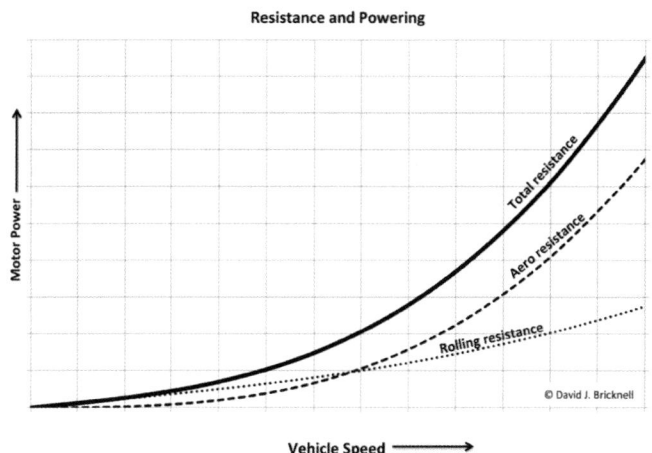

The illustration above is for a generic vehicle, CEV or BEV, showing the contributions from both rolling and aerodynamic drag:

Total Resistance is the sum of Rolling Resistance, Aerodynamic Resistance and Drive Train inefficiencies

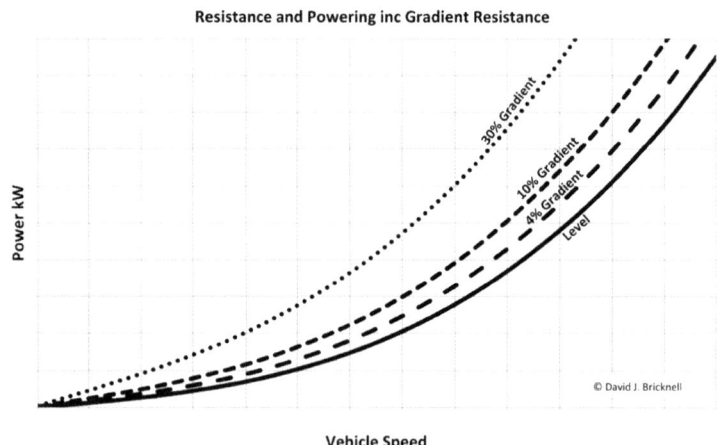

Hills have a significant impact on vehicle power requirements – the above chart shows the increase from typical motorway/highways, major trunk roads and other roads.

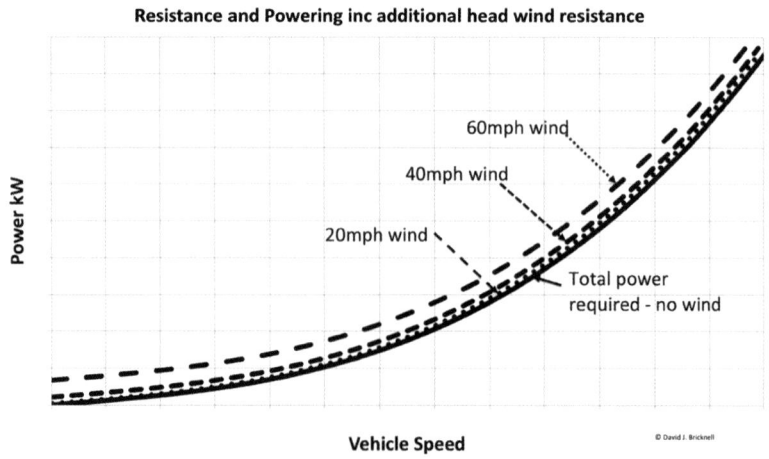

Strong head winds can also increase the power required to overcome the additional aerodynamic drag. Tail winds will reduce the power required by a similar amount.

Power (kW or hp) is a measure of force multiplied by speed – for an ICE or an electric motor this is torque multiplied by rpm.

The power curve for an CEV and an electric motor are quite different. Power is the product of torque and speed (motor or engine rpm). An electric motor can deliver maximum torque at zero rpm and it's this characteristic that allows a BEV to do without a clutch as it doesn't stall.

Due to the very wide power band achievable with today's electric motors, BEVs can manage with a single-stage fixed-gear whilst still delivering high power and rapid, smooth acceleration. A CEV on the other hand requires a clutch to ensure the engine doesn't stall as power is delivered to the wheels and requires multiple gears to ensure performance through the vehicle's speed range. See the illustration below.

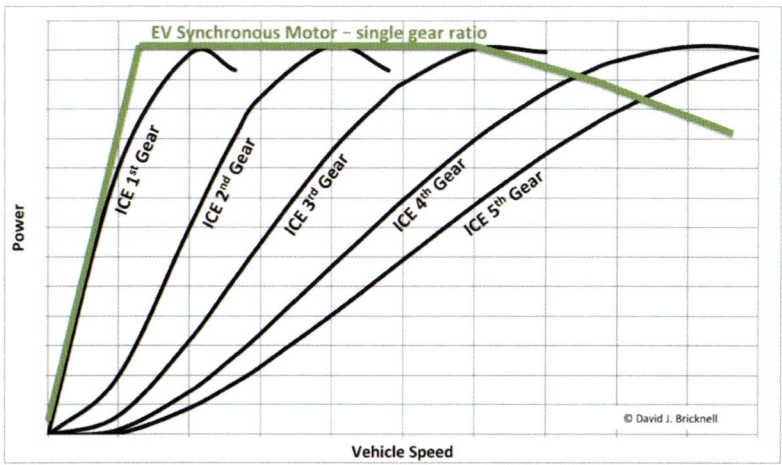

The chart shows the power curve at each gear step for a typical five speed CEV contrasted with a single-speed electric motor BEV.

Vehicle Weight

Early BEVs were generally heavier than a similar CEV but improved battery energy density and, in particular, purpose designed, not adapted from an CEV, electric vehicles have now narrowed the gap.

Some purpose designed BEVs are now lighter than their equivalent CEV. (Information from various manufacturers brochures).

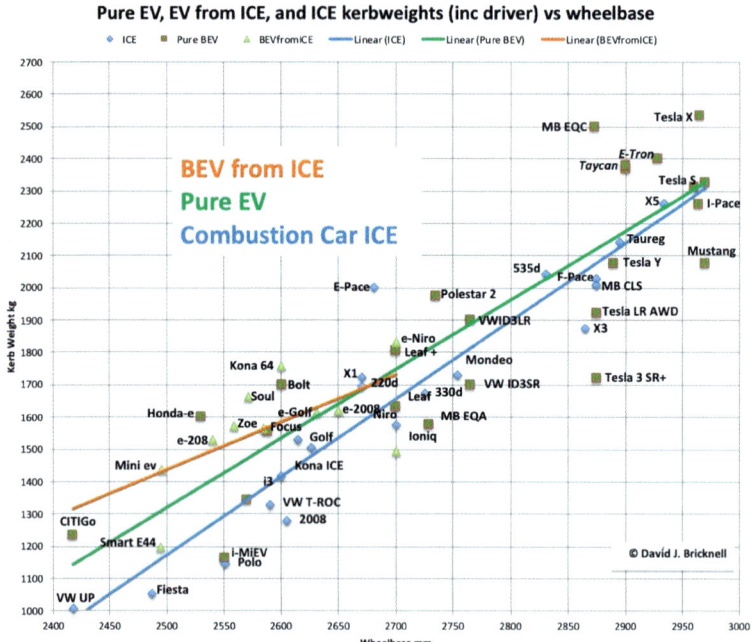

Chart showing Kerb or Curb Weight (including driver) against Wheelbase length for pure BEV, BEVs based on a CEV platform, and CEV. Trendlines are shown for each type.

Range

The range of a vehicle will depend upon how quickly it uses its stored energy (battery or fuel tank): energy is used to overcome resistance (rolling and aero), to overcome inefficiencies in the drivetrain (gears, bearings, etc.), to power the cars electronics, entertainment systems, lights, wipers, etc., to cool the cabin, and to heat the cabin (more significant for a BEV than an CEV).

Range will vary depending upon the driving style and the conditions for driving, including:

- the average and maximum speeds driven,

- the driving conditions – city, rural, motorway, etc., the road surface, as well as temperature, wind, rain and sun,

- the style of driving – relaxed or aggressive, accelerations and braking, stops and starts, etc.

BEV drivers vary in the type of range information they require depending upon their charging arrangements, their vehicle battery capacity, and their driving duty.

For a CEV, drivers normally 'fill the tank' and then drive until about a quarter tank remains before refilling either by a specific journey to a fuel station or as a detour from an existing journey. CEVs of the 1960s/70s, had an un-refuelled range of between 200 and 300 miles, but large-scale motorway/highway driving wasn't commonplace.

Today, 'official' range for CEVs can be 600miles or more on a single tank (based on tested mpg). An unintended consequence has been a reduction in the number of fuel stations, leading to longer journeys just to fill up – a particular problem for those in the less well populated and rural areas. [21]

An unintended and undesirable consequence of better fuel economy has been an increase in the attraction of larger, less fuel-efficient city-based Sports Utility Vehicles (SUVs). [22]

For a driver new to BEVs and expecting to treat them just like an CEV, they will often want to know how far they can drive before they have to recharge – on the basis of charge to full and recharge at 20% or so. This may also apply to those that don't have access to home, workplace or destination charging.

For most BEV drivers that have home charging, this is not a significant 'range' to know unless a single journey planned exceeds that which the battery is capable of – with an average daily mileage of 20miles (UK, 2017), this will not be a factor for many, if not most, drivers. [23] This is even more so the case with BEVs in 2020 and their increasingly longer ranges.

The two types of 'range' can then be quite different: one comprising of a lot of town driving, numerous stop-starts, some cold starts,; and the other, maybe, a single run at a motorway or highway speed of 70mph/110kph or whatever the prevailing country speed limits are.

'Real World' range therefore depends upon which world is real to you. It can be measured in many ways and each will be more meaningful to different BEV drivers.

Testing Protocols and 'Official' or 'Sticker' Range

In order to allow a like-for-like comparisons and for 'official' taxation purposes, countries require vehicles to be tested under strictly controlled laboratory conditions. In the USA there is the Environmental Protection Agency EPA test and for quite a bit of the rest of the world, the World harmonized Light vehicle Test Procedure or WLTP. Europe has now adopted the WLTP rather than the previous New European Driving Cycle NEDC which was widely derided as overoptimistic. Other countries also have their own testing procedures.

Both EPA and WLTP testing cycles provide a known baseline against which to compare different makes and models of vehicle. EPA testing includes a City, a Highway and a Combined efficiency and range whilst WLTP testing, from April 2020 onwards, includes a City and a Combined range.

Using a simple 'average' vehicle efficiency collected over a period of a year of driving from a variety of BEV owners (just recorded distance over energy used) indicates that drivers were achieving over a lifetime around 75% (within a range of 55 and 85%) of the range of the WLTP combined cycle and around 80% (within a range of 60 and 90%) of the EPA combined cycle. Clearly there is quite a large variation in peoples driving style, types of trips and terrain.

Replicating the testing cycle on the road is very difficult due to the accelerations and braking sequences required but where manufacturers have posted testing showing steady state consumption, these range figures can be achieved provided a fairly flat dry road in mild, calm conditions is available i.e. something that replicates the testing condition. The challenge is always holding to a lower speed (average 48mph or 55mph depending on the test) than is usual on a main highway or motorway.

EPA testing for BEVs varies a little from the CEV testing. The CEV testing includes City (or UDDS – Urban Dynamometer Driving Schedule) and Highway but also adds three other tests to account for: a cold start city cycle, more aggressive and faster driving (US06 – supplemental Federal Test Procedure), and air conditioning use (SC03 Supplemental Federal Test Procedure with Air Conditioning). Testing of BEVs on the other hand use a combination of the City/UDDS and Highway cycles but supplement this with a long duration steady state run at 55mph in order to fully deplete the battery.

The full test starts by charging the vehicle to full and then running through a sequence of Urban (7.5mi at average 19.6mi/h), Highway (10.26mi at average 48.3mph), Steady Speed (55mph) tests followed by a repeat Urban, Highway, Urban and a final steady state until the vehicle is unable to hold 55mph. It is then stopped, and the vehicle is recharged to full. The official range is then adjusted by a factor of typically 70% to represent driving in normal road conditions. Efficiency (including mpg equivalent) is determined by dividing the official range by the amount of recharge energy.

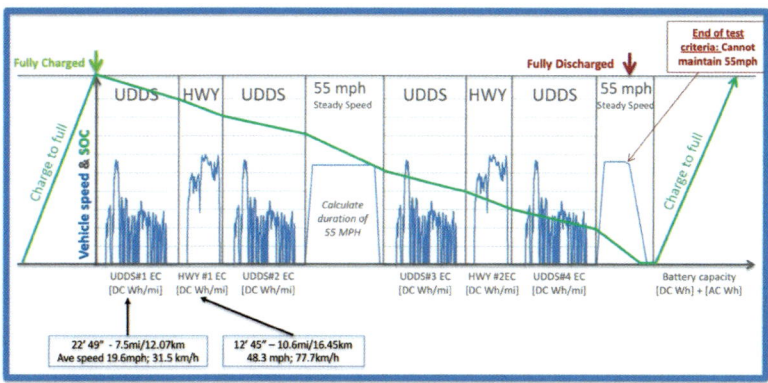

The chart above, adapted from a chart produced by ANL by Micael Duoba, Henning Lohse-Busch, Kevin Stutenberg, and Eric Rask provides a good visual illustration of the EPA BEV test

WLTP testing follows a similar procedure but, disappointingly, WLTP and EPA couldn't agree a common protocol.

The WLTP testing for cars (WLTP Class 3b) is based around four different test cycles – Low, Medium, High, and Extra High. The WLTP City test includes a Low and a Medium test. The Combined Test includes Low, Medium, High and Extra High.

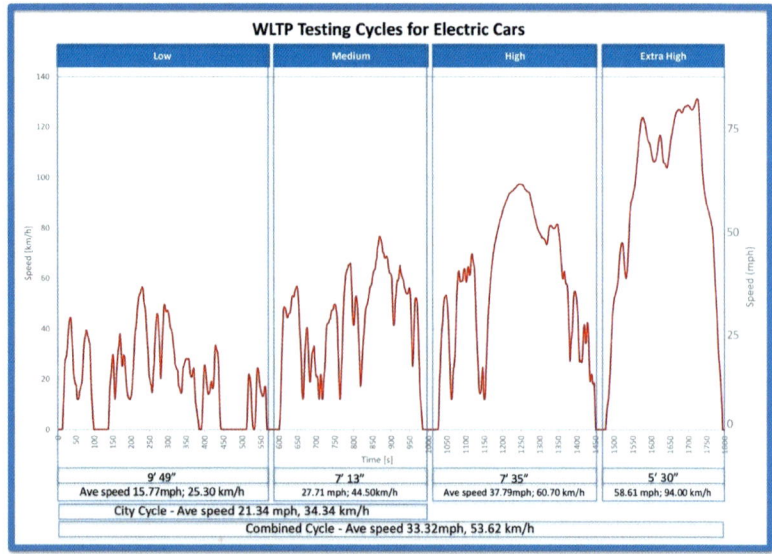

WLTP range testing involves charging to full and then running through each cycle in turn - Low and Medium for City or all four cycles for combined. The cycles are repeated until the car is unable to maintain the speed required for the cycle, regardless of which cycle that is. There is no high-speed steady state run.

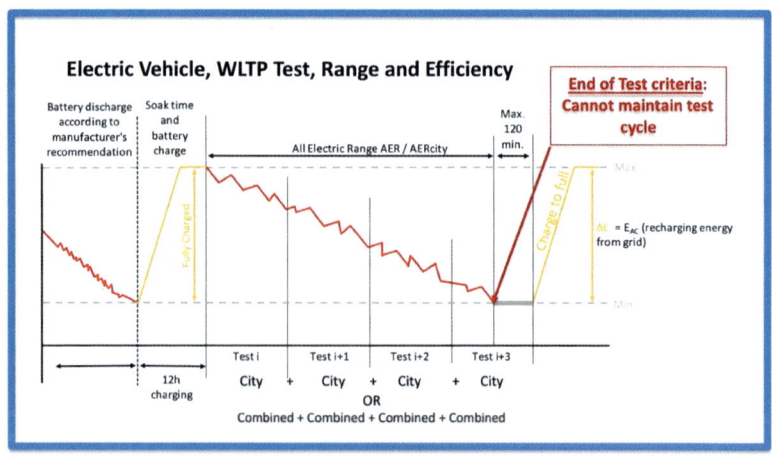

At first look, the testing for range, a significant criterium for BEVs even in 2020, look to be similar. Both City and Highway average speeds look quite similar. However, the Combined cycle average speeds are significantly different due to the EPA using a 55mph steady state run to deplete the battery whereas WLTP just repeats the all four cycles.

The table below illustrates this.

	Average Speeds mph	
	EPA	WLTP
City	21.20	21.34
Highway	48.30	46.66
Steady State	55.00	-
Combined	48.46	33.32
Note. EPA combined based on Tesla 3 AWD		

Table showing the average speeds for the two testing protocols, WLTP and EPA. Of course, the testing is not just about average speed, but speed is a significant factor. The combined range will differ between the two testing protocols. Shown in the table is the average combined speeds based upon a Tesla 3 LR AWD but the 55mph steady speed part of the test will vary based upon overall battery pack size.

Trade Magazine Testing and Independent Tests

EV range is also often tested by various trade magazines. They provide a different way of assessing 'real-world' range but are difficult to compare like-for-like as the conditions they are run in and the type of driving styles applied vary quite significantly.

BEV	Miles											
					Nextmove.de							
	EPA	WLTP	70mph (calc)	Tom Moloughney 70mph	72mph	75mph	81mph	Autocar/ Whatcar	CarWOW 5degC	minus 2 degC	Autobest	EV-Database
BMW i3 120	153	177-193	135					165		153	144	140
Audi e-Tron	204	249	214		187		171	196	206	212		235
Mercedes EQC	220	259	207					208	194	191		225
Leaf e+ Tekna	225	285	186	185				217	208	186		205
Jag I-Pace S	234	298	221			169		253	223	207	195	230
Bolt Mk1/Mk2	238	240	194/214	223 (Mk2)						184	234	
Renault Zoe 50		245	175					192		197		200
Kia e-Niro 64	239	282	196					253	255	224		235
Tesla M3 SR+	250	258	184					181				195
Kona 64	258	279	204		200		176	259		252		250
Tesla S SR	285	280	231					204				
Tesla 3 Perf	299	338	272					239				275
Tesla 3 LR AWD	322	348	283	289	252		222	211	270	251		285
Tesla X LR	325	315	243		254	242	223	233		261	249	285
Tesla S LR	370	375	303		298		266			292	263	325

Examples of "real-range" captured by various trade publications. They are all valuable but there is not 'one' range figure, it depends... [24 25 26 27 28 29 30]

Hypermiling [31]

With earlier BEVs there was some enthusiasm for depleting the battery at quite low speeds (20-40mph) in order to demonstrate the longest possible range. An interesting exercise but with the larger battery capacity of most new BEVs, and potential ranges of in excess of 1000miles at these very low speeds, this is something unlikely to be continued.

'Long Journey' Range

For those BEV drivers with larger battery capacities, the 'range' figure they are keen to know is how far they are likely to be able to drive between recharging when on a 'long journey' at highway or motorway speeds.

The analysis that follows will show the difference that can be expected by driving more slowly or more quickly, more aggressively or more leisurely, in colder, warmer or wetter conditions, and the variation that can be expected throughout the seasons. Much of the range variation applies equally to CEVs.

Longer range can be achieved in some BEVs by selecting an ECO driving mode instead of comfort. Depending on the BEV, ECO mode turns off heated seats, climate control, heated wheel, heated windshield and reduces blower or fan speed. Some manufacturers have a 'Range-Mode' which conditions the battery cells to allow maximum energy extraction.

Similarly, range may be impacted when a sportier mode is selected: manufacturers vary in describing their standard and ECO or Standard and Sport, or similar modes.

For a CEV, transmission inefficiency at lower speeds can be significant - modern CEVs usually have more than five gears ratios with some having up to nine. Combustion efficiency will reduce as rpm decreases. Cabin cooling using air conditioning does reduces range but heating of the cabin is done with waste combustion heat and hence doesn't impact range. An illustration of the power required and the matching range variation throughout the vehicle speed range is shown below – there is a little variation as one goes through the gears, but the solid line shows a smoothed curve.

Electric Vehicle Technologies

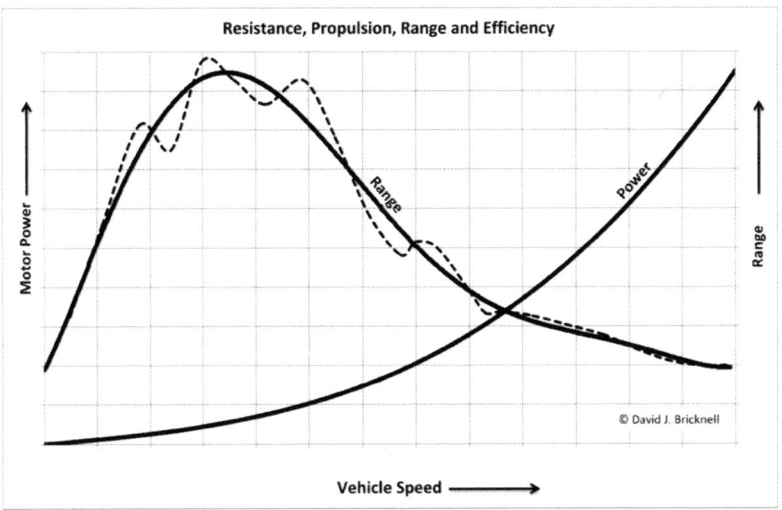

Resistance, Propulsion, Range and Efficiency

A range chart for a typical CEV would include the efficiency of the engine and transmission during each of the gear changes. Compared to a BEV the efficiency at lower speeds is much reduced and the peak efficiency occurs at a generally higher speed.

For a BEV the energy stored in the battery is used for motion, overcoming transmission inefficiency, electronics losses, cooling, and, because there is little waste heat from inefficiencies, also for heating the cabin. However, transmission inefficiency is considerably less for a BEV because they use a single locked-train gear often integrated with the differential rather than a multi-stage gear train.

Motor efficiencies are also high and motor efficiency at lower speeds remain particularly high when adopting permanent magnet motors that eliminate the energising losses of an induction motor.

In a number of new BEVs, two (or three) motors are used to further reduce drivetrain inefficiencies at lower speeds better matching power available to that demanded.

On a level road, the range curve for a BEV shows a peak at very low speeds decreasing as rolling resistance increases and reducing more rapidly as aerodynamic losses build up. Increasing aerodynamic resistance is the most significant contributor to reduced range at higher speeds for both CEV and BEV although there is a small contribution from loss of effective battery capacity due to a higher energy discharge rate (C-rate) at higher vehicle speeds.

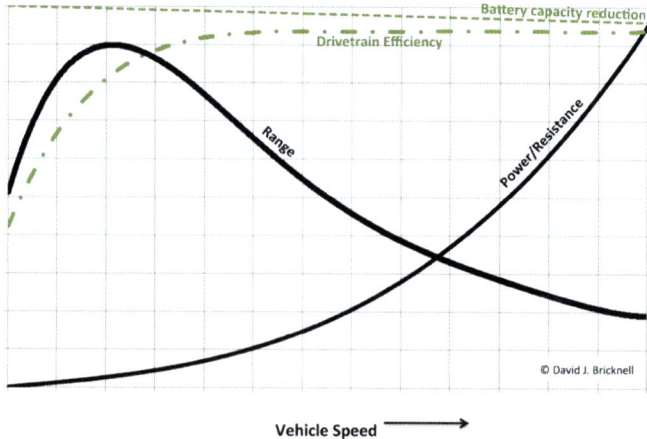

A range chart for a typical BEV includes the efficiency of the motor, inverter and transmission, as well as the battery capacity variation with discharge rate

Summary charts for 2020 BEVs

BEV manufacturers in 2020 take different views on vehicle weight and aerodynamics. Driver preferences and marketing play an important part in how the vehicle looks and this follows through on the power required and the efficiency and range achieved for a given battery pack size.

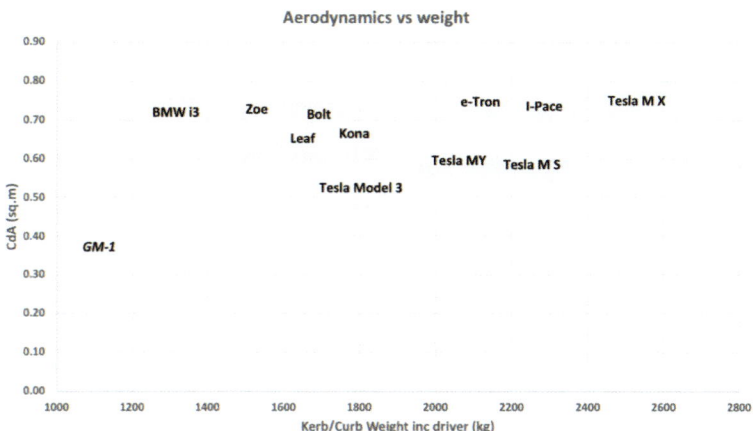

The impact of vehicle weight and aerodynamics on required power and on range can be seen in these charts. The baseline is the ultra-low weight and highly aerodynamic GM EV-1, an early BEV, much loved by those that lived with it,

GM's EV-1 – Lightweight and highly aerodynamic electric vehicle
(RightBrainPhotography (Rick Rowen) CC BY-SA 2.0

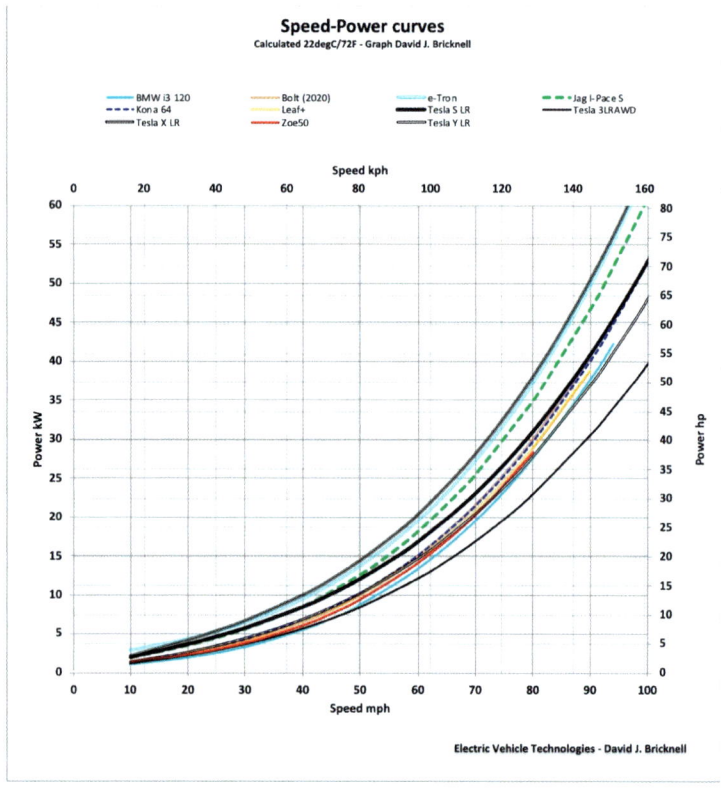

Speed-Power curves for some of the major BEVs in 2020.

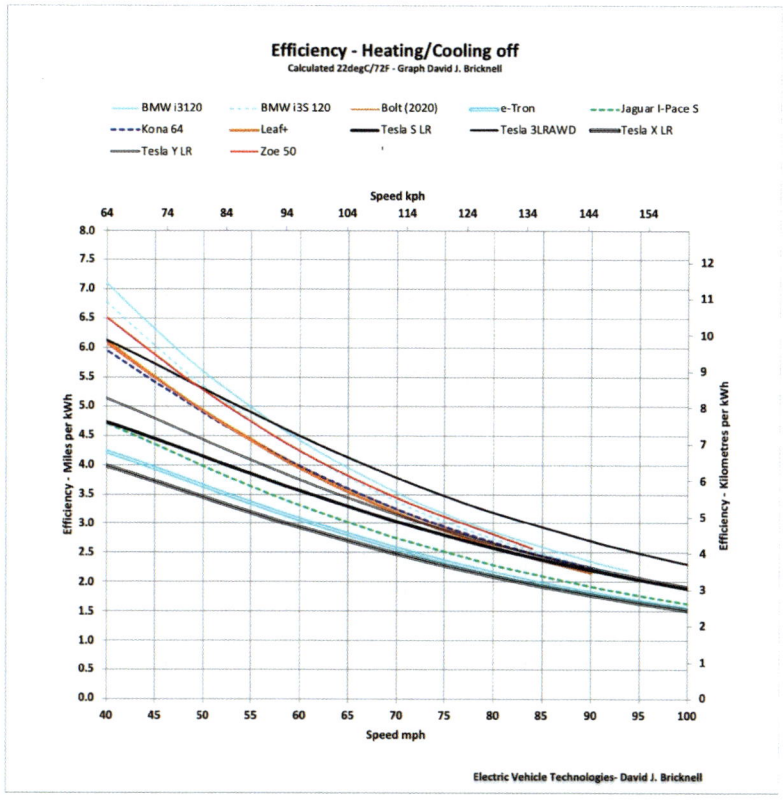

Speed-Efficiency curves for some of the major BEVs in 2020.

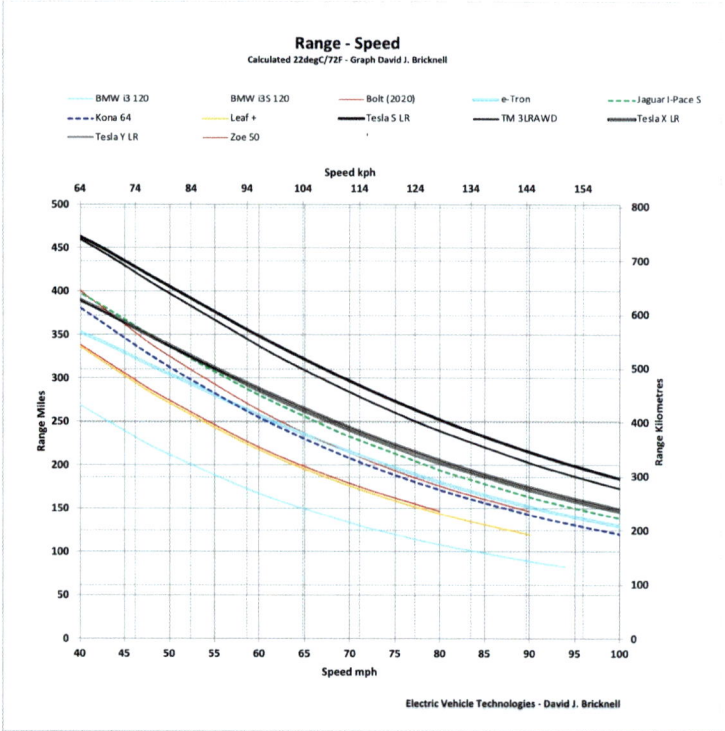

Speed-Range curves for some of the major BEVs in 2020.

Electric Vehicle Technologies

Weight and aerodynamics are the two key factors in determining efficiency at the varying different vehicle speeds – for a given battery capacity range will increase with increasing efficiency.

The chart below shows the effect of varying weight and aerodynamics (frontal area and drag coefficient).

The five vehicle types shown vary from a lightweight and aerodynamic car through lightweight but not aerodynamic, an aerodynamic saloon, and un-aerodynamic saloon and a large heavy SUV type.

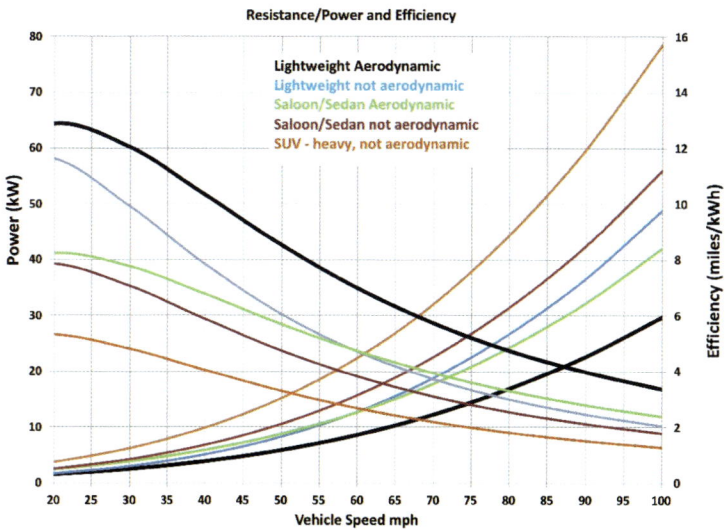

The Weather

The weather (sun, wind, rain, ambient temperature, etc.) affects all vehicles whether CEV or BEV.

A CEV is specifically affected by more idling, engine warm up, higher lubricant viscosity at cooler temperatures, and weaker petrol/gasoline.

For both CEV and BEV, lower ambient temperatures increase air density and hence increases aerodynamic resistance. Lower ambient temperatures also reduce tyre pressures which increases rolling resistance.

For warmer temperatures, losses due to cooling the cabin with air conditioning reduce range in both BEVs and in CEVs.

Cabin heating however is the area of significant difference to CEV. In order to heat the cabin, BEVs use battery energy either through resistive heating or a heat pump (reverse of a refrigeration system) but in both cases battery energy is used and hence range is reduced and, because heating is time related and propulsion is speed related, the speed at which peak range is achieved increases as ambient temperature reduces and cabin heating load increases. Cabin heating for an CEV makes use of waste heat from inefficient combustion and hence does not impact on range.

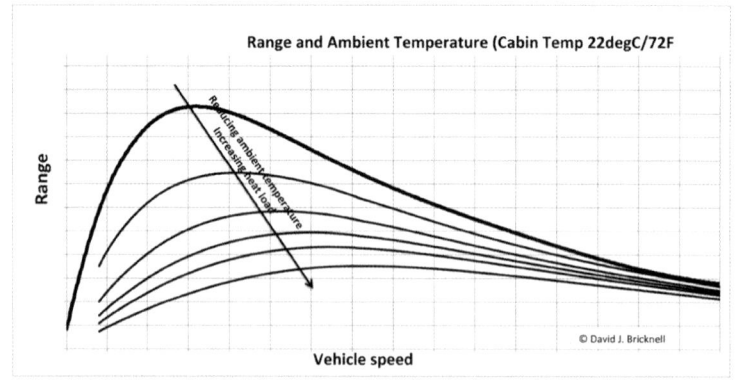

Chart showing the impact of ambient temperature variation on range throughout the vehicle speeds

This means that there will be a variation of expected range from a BEV throughout the year. The shape will depend upon whether its Northern Hemisphere or Southern Hemisphere and on whether it's a temperate climate or one with more extremes of weather.

This can be seen in the predicted or GOM range shown together with the maximum and minimum ambient temperatures throughout the months of the year. The term 'GOM' is one often used by BEV drivers and refers to the 'Guess' that a BEV makes of the available range for the day. Not all BEVs make this guess. Tesla, for instance, simply applies EPA combined cycle range pro-rata for battery SOC but, of course, once one enters a destination in the navigation system it makes its best estimate/guess of the available range.

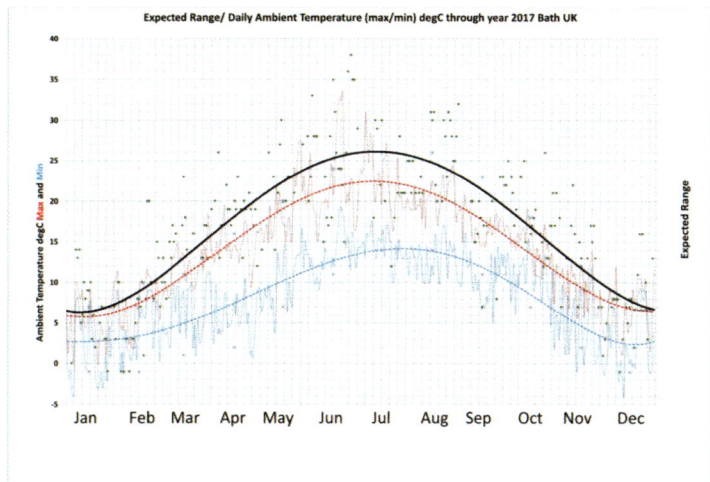

Range for a BEV tracks very closely against ambient air temperature. The chart above shows the predicted range throughout the year together with maximum and minimum ambient temperatures.

A comparison of range reduction due to ambient temperature effects can be seen in this chart showing a BEV against an ICE- Hybrid and a pure CEV (range set to equivalent).

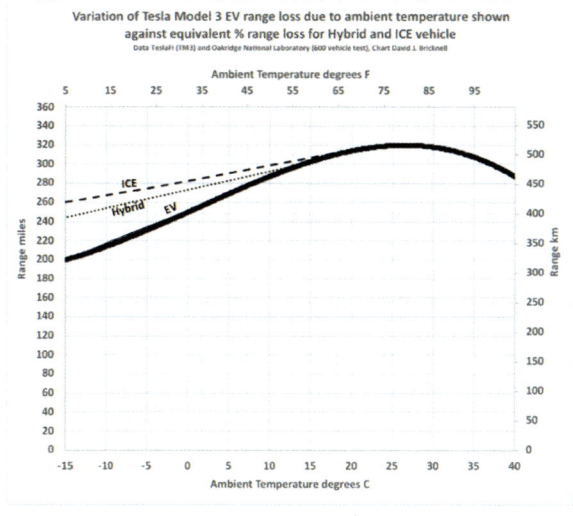

Impact of ambient temperature on CEV, PHEV and BEV. [32]
The data for CEV and hybrids came from Oakridge National Laboratories [33] *testing of 600 vehicles.*

Rain may or may not occur at the same time as lower temperatures, but the cooling impact of rain can be quite significant. Rain cools the tyres causing an increase in rolling resistance and well as using energy to accelerate the rain drops when hitting them. [34]

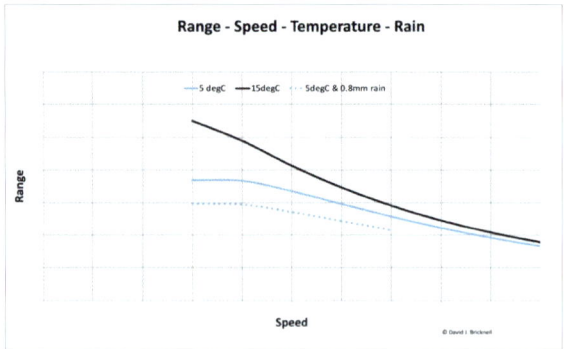

This chart shows just 0.8mm of water (5ºC), some way off the typical 2.5mm that aquaplaning might start to occur.

Range is also affected by driving style, route and road type: average speeds are higher on highways and motorways and slower with more acceleration and braking when driving in cities. Aggressive or enthusiastic driving will also affect range. Both CEV and BEVs are affected similarly if there is reduced opportunity to regenerate energy.

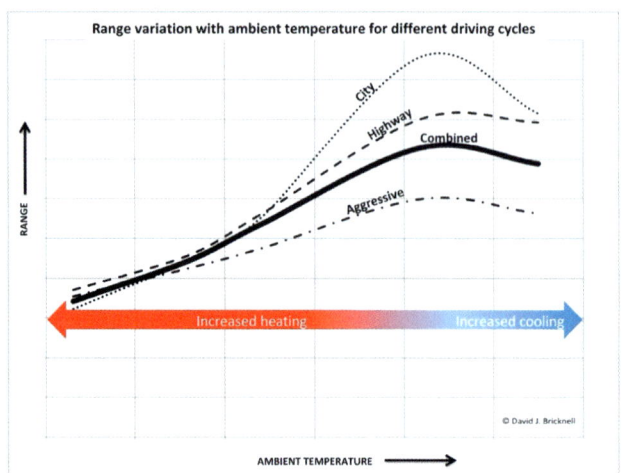

The chart shows the range variation from different driving cycles representing city and highway/motorway as well as an aggressive style and these are plotted against external ambient temperature with a comfortable target cabin temperature. Data based on a series of BEV tests by Advanced Vehicle Testing Facility.

The graph combines the contribution of four things to the reduction in range due to ambient temperature change.

The battery capacity is reduced as Li-Ion batteries are less willing to give up charge when cold, but this is quite small compared to the heating energy usage.

There is an increase in vehicle drag due to increased air density although can be quite small compared to the other factors.

There is an increase in rolling resistance due to colder tyres.

The largest change comes from the heating or cooling load. BEVs have little or no waste heat with which to heat the cabin and have to generate it either from a resistive heating coil or from a heat-pump.

A heat pump can help to reduce heating load. Simply installed, the efficiency of the heat pump will reduce as the difference in temperature of the ambient air compared to the refrigerant temperature narrows. Many BEVs are now use the waste heat from the motor and inverter cooling, and even the battery mass, to improve heat pump performance at very low ambient temperatures. Increasingly, this is an area of considerable complexity and is becoming a differentiator in vehicle performance.

Preconditioning an BEV whilst plugged-in will help range mostly by warming or cooling the cabin and by warming the battery: preheating the battery does make a small difference in battery capacity but a quite significant range improvement can be made because energy can be regenerated into a warmer battery from the beginning of the journey.

Given the impact of heating on a BEV's range there is quite evidently a difference in achievable range throughout the year- the extent of which depends upon variation in ambient temperatures throughout the year.

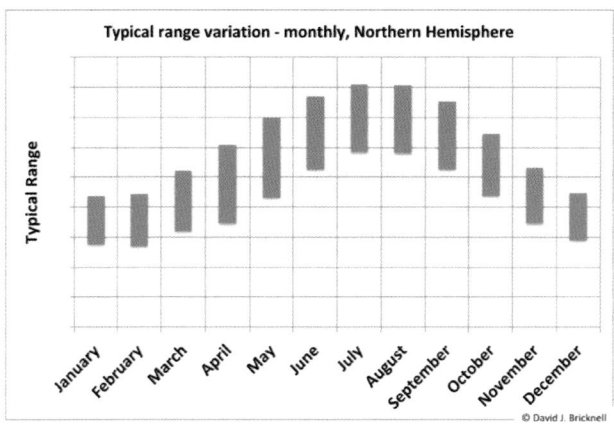

Variation in range throughout the year (Northern Hemisphere).

Acceleration and maximum continuous speed

Those new to BEVs are always surprised to find how easy they are to drive quickly: instant torque, no gear changes and high excess-power all contribute to a very spirited drive.

With some BEVs, maximum speed can be rather more restricted than in a comparable CEV although normally still in excess of most maximum speed limits. Recent BEVs with large battery capacities are now achieving the sort of maximum speeds comparable to the fastest CEV.

Three things will normally contribute to the BEVs maximum speed:

- Motor continuous power (can be around half of the rated maximum power);

- Inverter continuous power (again can be considerably less than the rated maximum power);

- battery discharge rate (typically 1-C for continuous, 2-C limited time, and maybe up to 8-C for acceleration power).

These operating envelopes are shown on the chart below

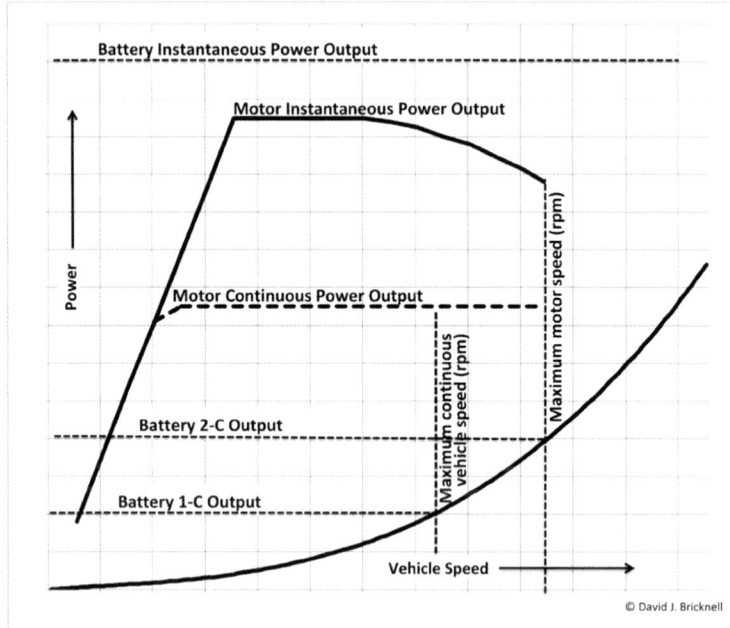

© David J. Bricknell

Cooling of these components is essential for sustaining high power / high speeds or for aggressive driving involving high acceleration and sharp braking. The Battery Management System BMS will reduce power available from the battery if sustained high discharge rates are likely to impact on battery life.

Inverter cooling can be critical and Tesla's move to SiC-MOSFETs in place of IGBTs is something many performance related BEV manufacturers will no doubt follow. Motor temperatures can also be a determining factor. Both components can cause a reduction in available power if a lot of acceleration and braking causes high component temperatures.

Driving Styles and Regeneration

How a BEV is driven has a considerable impact on battery capacity and vehicle range as well as on battery life. One area where BEVs differ from CEVs is in their ability to regenerate driving energy back into the battery: in city driving cycles in warmer weather this can recover up to 40% energy although when on a motorway or highway the opportunity for regeneration is typically less than 10% energy.

When the battery is very cold, regeneration is restricted or denied by the battery management system to avoid cell damage.

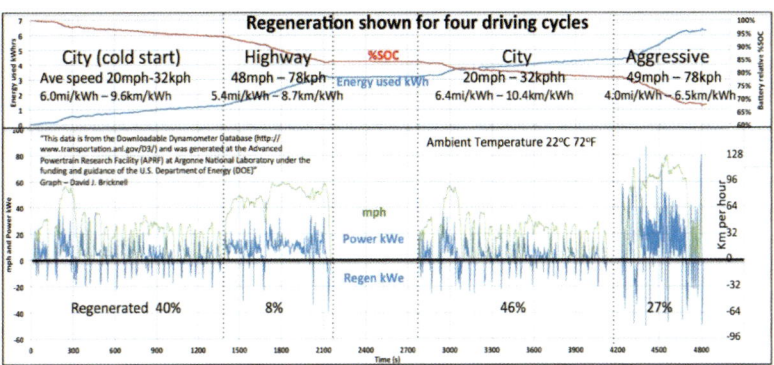

This chart shows the impact of different driving cycles on the rate of energy usage for a BEV. Cold and hot start city driving is shown as well as highway and aggressive driving. Regeneration during each of the four different driving cycles can be seen – during highway driving regen contributes little but during city driving it can be a quite significant range-improving energy-saving measure.[35]

This next chart shows a cold-start city cycle against a hot start and the additional energy used on a cold start can be clearly seen. Some of this comes from additional heating load and that can be seen in the small disparity between the hot (in red) and cold (in blue) power and some from the fact that BEVs won't regenerate power back into the battery either at high battery SOC or at low battery temperatures - tests at -17°C/1F show the battery didn't receive any regenerated energy until some 20 minutes of city driving losing some 10% of potential recoverable energy in this test at this very low temperature.

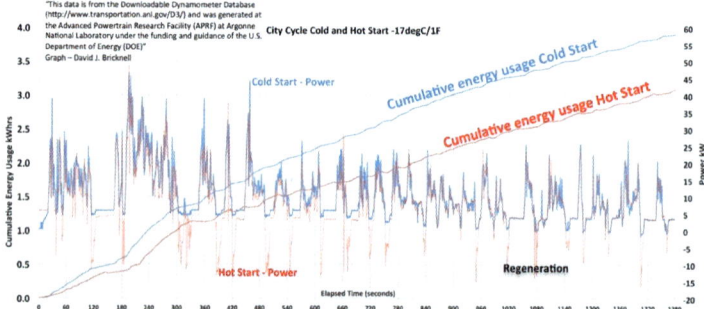

Regenerated energy comparison between cold and hot start city driving cycles – the battery management system BMS prevents regenerating until the battery cells have warmed from driving.

Emissions

Emissions

One of the many reasons for driving a BEV is to reduce the impact on the environment, particularly in towns and cities.

In assessing the impact of transport and energy generation on the environment and on the population at large there is often confusion between Green House Gases GHGs and Toxic Emissions.

Global Warming and Green House Gases

Anthropogenic global warming is occurring due to the 'Greenhouse' effect of global warming gases in the atmosphere. Global Warming occurs from the Green House effect where Global Warming Gases trap heat in the atmosphere - there has been a significant increase in CO_2 in the atmosphere since the Industrial Revolution.[36]

The Global Warming Potential (GWP) of Greenhouse Gases (GHGs) include Carbon Dioxide CO_2 (GWP=1), Methane (~56x), and Nitrous Oxide NO (~280x) as well as Hydrofluorocarbons HFCs (up to 10,000x).[37]

Nitrous Oxide N_2O (rather than Nitrogen dioxide NO_2) mostly comes from agriculture (about 75% from both nitrogen fixing in the soil and animal waste) but some (about 10%) also comes from vehicle emissions. [38] Nitrous Oxide is colourless, non-toxic, and non-flammable, but has a GWP of some 300 times that of CO_2.

Methane is produced naturally in wetlands, is manmade by energy (gas and coal extraction), and also comes from ruminants (cows and sheep) and decaying matter. [39] It has a GWP of some 20-70 times that of CO_2 but is not as abundant.

Carbon Dioxide CO_2 is some 200 times more abundant than Methane, which is why it makes a larger contribution to Global Warming even though its GWP is lower. CO_2 is not defined as a toxic gas (although some occupations (brewers and miners) are at risk from high concentrations of CO_2. Dangerous concentrations are considered to be some 150 times atmospheric levels. CO_2 occurs naturally but combustion of fossil fuels for electricity, transportation and in industry is increasing the amount of CO_2 in the atmosphere at a rate that is accelerating Global Warming. [40]

Toxic Emissions

Toxicity, on the other hand, is dose (or concentration) dependent: the impact of the toxic emission is not detectable below a certain level and then once above that level toxicity increases as concentration increases.[41]

For vehicles, the key toxic emission of most concern is Nitrogen Dioxide (NOx). High NOx levels are related to a significant number of early deaths.[42]

Internal Combustion Engines also emit Particulates PMs (soot and other fine particles)[43]. Particulates are toxic and are categorized as:

- PM_{10} (coarse 10μm to 2.5μm) these will reach into the upper respiratory tract,

- $PM_{2.5}$ (fine 2.5μm to 1μm) these will reach into the lower respiratory tract,

- PM_1 (inhalable 1μm to 0.1μm) these will reach deep into the alveoli, in the lungs where gas exchange takes place,

- $PM_{0.1}$ (ultra-fine <0.1μm) are the most hazardous and can reach into the bloodstream and whole body including crossing the placenta.

Diesel and now gasoline Particulate Filters DPF don't always catch many of these fine and ultra-fine particles and because of their very small size they tend not to produce visible smoke. [44]

Particulates are harmful at any concentration and can penetrate deep into the lungs and ultra-fine particles can cross from the lungs into the blood stream, including crossing to the foetal side of the placenta. The finer the particle the more hazardous it is. "Exposure to particles can lead to mortality (death), increased admissions to hospital of people suffering from cardiovascular (heart) disease (attacks and strokes), and pulmonary (lung) disease, such as Chronic Obstructive Pulmonary Disease (COPD), bronchitis and asthma. Other compounds found on particulates, such as some hydrocarbons or metals, can cause cancer or poisoning." [45] [46]

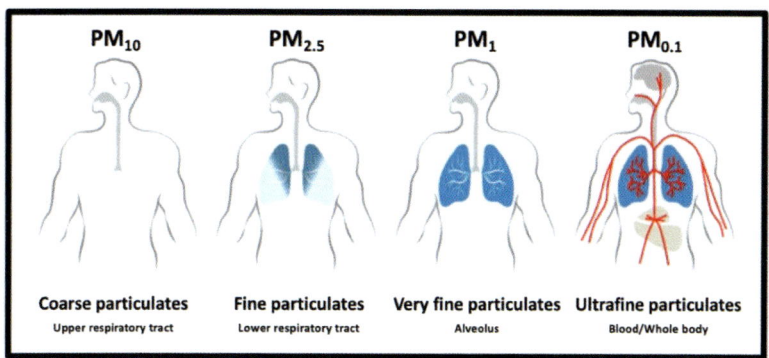

Penetration into the body of particulates [47]

Tyre and brake particles can be substantially reduced by regenerative braking and smoother acceleration and deceleration, something that is a characteristic of electric vehicles. Many reports refer to an early assessment of vehicle tyre and brake dust that assumed BEVs were some 25% heavier than a similar CEV. This weight difference is certainly no longer the case with many of the latest BEVs matching the weights of similar CEV. No allowance was made for regenerative braking avoiding friction brake usage something that substantially reduces brake pad wear. More research is underway. [48]

Diesels are two to five times worse on NOx emissions than petrol/gasoline engines - this is a function of higher combustion temperatures and pressures. Increasing efficiency by increasing the combustion temperatures of the engine reduces CO_2 but increases NOx. Further increasing efficiency of the engine by lean-burn (using less fuel) renders the previously used three-way catalytic converter non-functional but does then require a lean NOx trap.

As well as the lean NOx trap, other methods for reducing NOx emissions include Exhaust Gas Recirculation EGR (which reduces combustion temperature but in doing so increases particulates) or Selective Catalytic Reduction SCR (using injected Urea or AdBlue into the exhaust catalyst) but this drops the engine efficiency thereby increasing CO_2.

Some engines are adopting a Miller Cycle to further reduce NOx whilst not increasing PMs or lowering efficiency; the Miller cycle reduces combustion temperature by closing the intake valve early and expanding the compressed gas hence cooling it (Charles Law) but in order to regain power and efficiency requires expensive two-stage turbocharging to increase charge density.

Petrol/gasoline engines use the Otto Cycle and are lower in NOx (because combustion temperatures are lower) but higher in CO_2 (because efficiency is lower) but they produce much fewer Particulates (unless they use Gas Direct Injection GDI).

Diesels use a direct-injection, compression-ignition, 'diesel-cycle' and produce more PMs. PMs used to be just a diesel problem but in order to reduce CO_2 and improve engine efficiency, petrol/gasoline engines are now adopting Gas Direct Injection GDI which has increased particulate emissions.

For all Power Stations, including Coal, NOx levels are lower per kWhr than Internal Combustion Engines. Gas fired power generation produces about a third of the NOx produced by coal. Coal and oil-fired power stations will produce Sulphur Dioxides SOx as well as toxic heavy metals (mercury, lead, cadmium, etc.) which burning gas doesn't[49]. Gas has typically 10,000 times fewer PMs than coal.

Power Stations are generally away from town centres whereas vehicle emissions are at their most concentrated, and hence most toxic, in town centres. Emissions at the point of use are an important factor for the concentration of toxic emissions but not for CO_2.

In summary, containing CO_2 (a GHG) is important to the future of the planet and, through taxation, lower CO_2 emissions directly affect vehicle purchase, but CO_2 isn't toxic.

A BEV CO_2 footprint will be lower than for an CEV and, on a like-for-like vehicle basis, the CO_2 associated with new vehicle manufacture will quickly be paid back in a couple of years or so. [50]

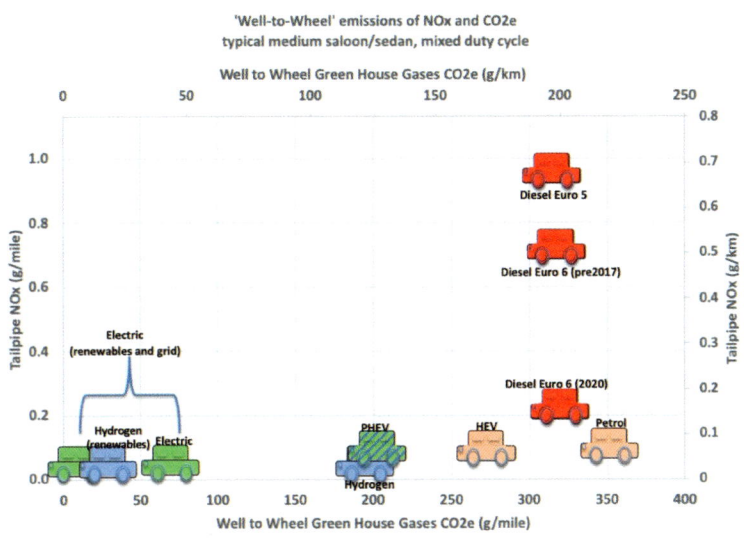

Tailpipe NOx and Well-to-Wheel CO2 for typical mid-sized saloon/sedan car [51]

This page left intentionally blank

Battery

Overview

The Lithium-Ion Battery (LIB) has probably been the single most influential development in the reintroduction of credible electric vehicles capable of challenging the dominance of ICE powered vehicles. In the last five to ten years energy density, specific energy, and cycle life have come together with significant cost reductions to make LIBs the energy storage of choice for BEVs.

Most consumer electronics use LIBs with a cathode of Lithium Cobalt Oxide (LCO), and, whereas some BEVs adopted Lithium Manganese Oxide (LMO) most chose Lithium Nickel Oxides, such as: Nickel Cobalt Aluminium (NCA), and Nickel Manganese Cobalt (NMC or sometimes written as NCM).

Heavier duty applications such as buses and trucks and marine vessels are also using Lithium Iron Phosphate (LFP) for long life or Lithium Titanate Oxide (LTO) where very rapid and frequent recharging is required however cost reductions of automotive NMC cells means marine is now looking at NMC whilst automotive are now looking again at LFP.

LIB cells are available in different formats with cylindrical, prismatic and pouch formats being used by different manufacturers. Battery packs are put together in strings of cells in series to get higher voltage and, where necessary, several parallel strings of series cells in order to get capacity.

Battery capacity isn't such an absolute value in the way that we perceive a tank of fossil fuel to be; the available capacity will depend upon the cell temperature and the rate of discharge amongst other things.

Batteries lose capacity through life, partly due to calendar ageing and partly due to charge/discharge cycling. The Battery Management System will seek to minimize damage the cycle life by restricting performance in lower or very high temperatures including reducing charging rate where necessary. Precondition of the battery in very cold weather is a user strategy for improving cell life. Cell balancing is essential to maintaining battery pack capacity.

For the future, improvements in anode and cathode materials are expected to lead to increased energy storage, improved rates of charging and increased cycle life. Considerable efforts are being made to introduce a solid electrolyte that would improve passive safety of the cell, improve cycle life and decrease charging time.

BEVs with larger battery packs (>60kWhrs) largely solve the problems of cycle life simply by needing less charging cycles for the same number of miles or kilometres per vehicle life – BEV battery life is now likely to be in the hundreds of thousands of miles or km. The million-mile battery life is not so far away. [52]

BEVs tend to use either a skateboard type configuration, where the battery pack is a flat structure extending the width of the car and between the wheelbase, or, particularly where a car shares a platform with an CEV, a configuration where cells are packaged in groups around the floor-pan, under the seats and anywhere else space can be found.

Some BEVs were once designed to enable quick battery swap [53]. The vehicle would drive into an on-route service area where it would be hoisted up, the cooling system drained, and the pack unbolted. A fresh charged pack would then be installed in its place, the cooling system refilled and the BMS reset before the car would continue on its journey. Rapid and ultra-rapid charging has rendered this idea obsolete.

Earlier battery packs consisted of modules containing a number of cells. Should the battery lose capacity then the pack could be then be removed and one module replaced. Such has been battery reliability that battery packs are now much more integrated into the vehicle structure and replacement would take a similar time to an CEV engine replacement.

The majority of battery packs operate at a nominal voltage of around 360V with a 400V maximum – one or more parallel arrangements of 96 cells in series. This has enabled BEVs to adopt the most generally available electrical systems and equipment. Some BEVs have now moved to 108 cells in series for a maximum 450V system and a few are now using an 800V/850V system. One can expect higher voltages to be used in the future in order to reduce weight and cooling requirements.

Different BEV manufacturers define battery capacity in different ways. Some restrict use of the top and bottom 10% leaving the remaining 80% to be redefined as '100%' – this removes the need for the driver to manage the charging profile. Others allow access to the full capacity but 'recommend' not regularly charging beyond 90% and warning when the battery reaches 20% SOC.

Battery Types

Battery technology has been one of the key improvements allowing for the wider adoption of Electric Vehicles. With little competition from the early 'explosion engines', BEVs, by the turn of the 20th century made up about a third of all cars on the road. These early BEVs were all of Lead-Acid type and had the benefit of being very easy to drive.

Lead-Acid batteries are heavy but, because BEVs were relatively slow, decent range was achieved on a single charge. Recharging a Lead-Acid battery is slow but with the small capacity of the BEVs batteries, overnight charging was acceptable.

Limited electricity infrastructure, improvements in the 'explosion engine' better known now as the internal combustion engine (ICE), improvements to the road infrastructure inviting longer ranges, faster vehicles, and cheaper mass-produced CEVs led to the end of the first age of the electric vehicle despite Edison's introduction of a much improved Nickel-Iron (NiFe) battery. [54]

NiFe was developed by Waldemar Jungner in 1899 but was much improved in 1901 by Thomas Edison. It had a much longer life than Lead-Acid and half the recharge time but was more expensive and so made BEVs even less competitive with CEVs.

Waldemar Junger, the inventor of the Nickel Iron battery also developed the Nickel Cadmium NiCd battery in 1899. As well as high discharge rates without losing capacity they have good low temperature performance and good cycle life but do suffer from 'memory' effect and, as cadmium is highly toxic, cadmium is now banned except in some medical and military applications.

In the 1960s, whilst some short-range Lead-Acid BEVs appeared (Henney Kilowatt [55], Scamp [56], and the Enfield 8000 [57]) others produced cars with different, albeit unsuccessful, battery technologies. GM's Electrovair [58] used Silver-Zinc (very high energy density but expensive and with low cycle life), and Amitron [59] used an innovative hybrid Lithium Nickel Flouride / NiCd (very high energy density but very poor power release from the Lithium Nickel Flouride was supplemented by the sustained high discharge rate of Nickel-Cadmium NiCd).

In the 1990s, Lead-Acid, NiCd, and even Ni-Fe batteries were used in some of the few BEVs of that generation, (GM EV1 Gen1 [60] and the Ford Ranger EV [61]) but others explored other battery chemistries. The Honda EV+ [62], released in 1988, used NiMH as did the GM EV1 Gen2, Toyota's RAV4 EV and a version of the Ford Ranger. Nickel-Metal Hydride NiMH was developed in 1967 and has a much higher energy density than NiCd.

NiMH has a high energy density than NiCd, and a better cycle life and shelf life and gave BEVs a credible driving range although recharge time remained quite slow.

Lithium Ion batteries were first proposed by British chemist M Stanley Whittingham during the 1970s whilst working for Exxon, but his Lithium-Titanium di-sulphide battery proved to be impractical. Ned Godshall (1979) and separately John Goodenough and Koichi Mizushima (1980) both demonstrated Lithium Cobalt Oxide LCO cells operating in the 4V range. Goodenough, Whittingham and Mizushima were awarded the Nobel prize in Chemistry in 2019 for developing Lithium Ion Batteries.[63]

Sony introduced the first commercial Lithium Ion cell in 1991 for use in consumer electronics and it has since displaced many other battery types due to its high cell voltage, its high energy and power density, and today, its ever-lower cost. [64]

Nissan produced the first Li-Ion battery powered EV, the Altra [65], in 1997 and whilst the Gen2 GM1, Toyota RAV4EV and Fords Ranger EV used NiMH, all future BEVs were to use variants of the Li-Ion battery. Nissan used Lithium Manganese Oxide - a chemistry they were to carry forward through their early versions of the Leaf range.

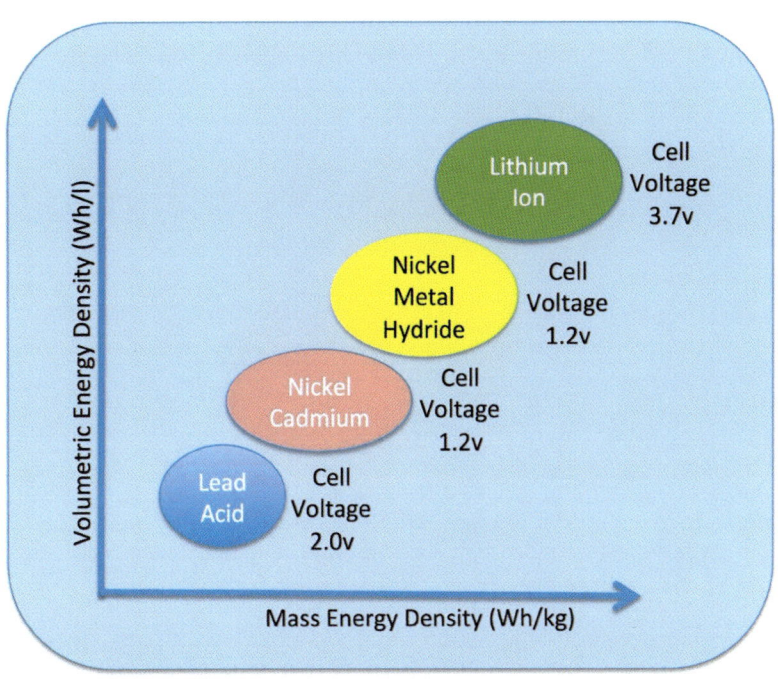

Lithium Ion Batteries can be significantly smaller and lighter than other rechargeable battery technologies and, importantly, have a much higher nominal cell voltage.

Lithium is the lightest metal, and the third lightest element; it also has the lowest reduction potential and hence the highest possible cell potential (voltage). However, the lithium ion battery is more a Nickel-Carbon battery that uses lithium ions to produce power.

A Lithium-Ion Battery (LIB) has an anode, a cathode, a separator, and an electrolyte.

An Ion is a particle (atom or molecule) with a net electrical charge. A LIB works by passing lithium ions between the electrodes through an electrolyte solution. The ions are 'intercalated' into the layered structure of the anode or cathode depending upon whether the battery is charging or discharging. Intercalation is described as "chemical reactions wherein lithium is inserted into a host matrix with essential retention of the crystal structure".[66]

As lithium ions move from the anode to the cathode it generates power. For recharging, the lithium ions move from the cathode to the anode. Intercalation is a reversible process.

The Anode is most often Graphite (except LTO) and the Cathode is composed of a mixed metal (NMC, LMO, NCA, etc.). Varying the anode/cathode composition leads to different battery characteristics. The electrolyte is normally a salt - lithium hexafluorophosphate - together with a mix of carbonates.

The separator is either a polymeric membrane, a fabric mat, or sometimes a ceramic.

Typical Li-Ion battery showing the current, electron and Ion flow during charging and discharging.

The **Solid Electrolyte Interphase** SEI is important for any of the LIBS using carbon anodes (most, except LTO). The SEI forms on first use of the battery and prevents the acid electrolyte from dissolving the carbon whilst still allowing ions through. During the life of the battery the SEI will thicken making the ion transfer (intercalation) more difficult and hence reducing the battery capacity. High charge/discharge rates and low temperature charge/discharge will thicken the SEI layer more rapidly. [67]

Battery Terminology

Rated Capacity, Energy, Energy Density, Specific Energy, C-Rate, State of Charge, State of Health, Depth of Discharge, and Cycle are terms that are commonly used when describing batteries.

Rated Capacity – expressed in Amp-hours or Ah and is the current (Amps) that can be delivered continuously from full to empty in a period of one-hour.

Energy – is the Rated Capacity at the battery nominal voltage measured in Watt hours or Wh. Watt is a measurement of power and is current multiplied by voltage – Amps x Volts. Nominal voltage is an average voltage over the battery discharge. For example, one Amp at two Volts discharged over one hour is 2Wh whereas 2-Amps at 2V over an hour is 4Wh.

C-rate – is the rate of discharge related to the rated capacity. A 10Ah battery at 1C delivers 10A for one-hour whereas a 10Ah battery at 4C delivers 10A for 15 minutes.

State of Charge – expressed as a percentage % of the full battery. Often, for the driver's benefit, the %SOC is a % of the net usable capacity rather than the gross capacity.

Depth of Discharge – DoD is the difference between the %SOC beginning and %SOC at the end of the discharge prior to recharging.

Cycle – is a discharge and recharge to the same SOC. Battery cycle life is the number of cycles from full to empty and back to full. Partial discharge and charge cycles can be summed to make a full cycle.

State of Health – is a measure of the current battery capacity compared to the battery capacity when new.

Two other measures are useful when comparing batteries.

Energy Density –is the amount of energy within a specific volume of battery.

Specific Energy – is the amount of energy within a specific mass (or weight) of battery.

Li-Ion Battery Chemistry

The principal LIB designations are: LCO, NCA, LMO, NMC, and LFP - these refer to the cathode composition. LTO is the other significant designation. All apart from LTO use a metal or mixed-metal cathode and a graphite anode; LTO uses a metal (titanate) anode and a mixed metal cathode.

For BEVs the following spider diagram shows the battery chemistries against five key parameters (4 is best, 1 is worst):

- Energy Density – how much energy (Wh) in a specific space and/or weight.

- Power Density – how quickly the energy can be released.

- Life – how many times it can be cycled.

- Cost – highest score is least expensive.

- Safety – likelihood of a thermal runaway.

-

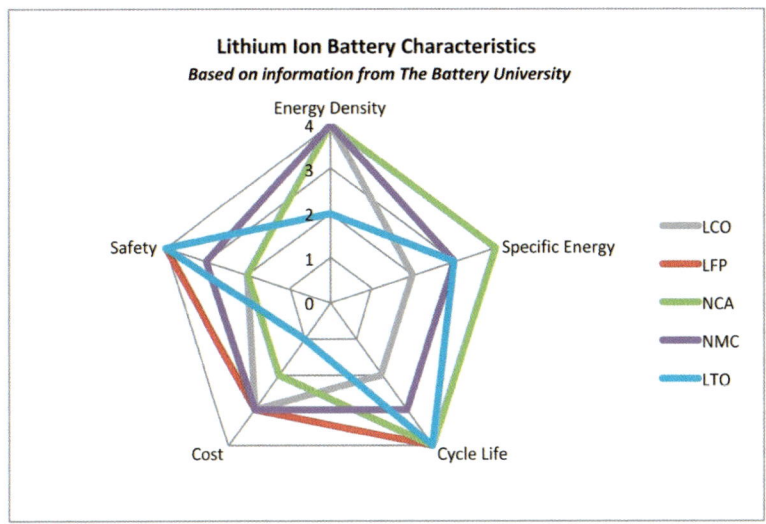

Li-Ion battery characteristics for various cathode chemistries. [68]

Major LIB Types

Lithium Cobalt Oxide LCO/Graphite is used in most consumer electronics. It has a Lithium Cobalt Oxide cathode and a graphite anode. It has a good cycle life and energy density but poor power density. It is expensive and has a higher likelihood of thermal runaway. It is not used for BEVs

Lithium Ferrous (Iron) Phosphate LFP/Graphite has a Lithium Ferrous Phosphate cathode and a graphite anode. It has excellent safety and good cycle life but has lower energy and power density as well as a lower cell voltage (3.2V). It has been a favoured technology for 'long-duration between charges' bus and coaches and for marine ferries that can charge only once per day. It avoids the use of Cobalt (expensive) and Nickel (supply constrained). Tesla have indicated that they will use LFP in their new lower range BEVs from China.

Mixed-Metal (NMC or NCA)/Lithium Titanate Oxide LTO use a mixed-metal cathode and a lithium titanate metal anode (unlike the other LIB variants) giving it a very fast charge rate, due to the very high surface area from the anode titanate nano-crystals and lack of SEI. LTO offers a wide operating temperature and a very high cycle life but a low energy density and a low cell voltage can lead to a high initial battery cost per kWh. LTO is considered very safe and is gaining favour for buses and ferries that are configured to charge very frequently (every hour or sometimes even more frequently).

Lithium Manganese Oxide LMO/Graphite use a Lithium Manganese Oxide cathode and a graphite anode. It does not use Cobalt and is hence less expensive. It is a safer alternative to LCO, but it has a lower cycle life. Nissan's early Leaf used LMO batteries but suffered somewhat from high temperature degradation issues [69]. Many early BEVs mixed LMO with NMC. The LMO provided the high current boost for acceleration with the NMC providing the longer endurance.

Nickel Manganese Cobalt NMC/Graphite uses a Nickel Manganese Cobalt cathode and a graphite anode. NMC is better suited to Pouch type cells than NCA due to NCA's propensity to generate more gas as it degrades. As most BEVs other than Tesla have adopted Pouch type cells then NMC has become the most commonly adopted chemistry. Manufacturers have developed NMC (also known as NCM) from NMC_{111} where each metal is a third of the cathode to the more power dense Nickel-rich NMC_{622}. Nickel-Rich NMC has gained significant interest recently both because it reduces the amount of expensive cobalt but also because it has the potential for a higher cell voltage and hence increasing energy density. NMC_{721}, NMC_{811}, and $NMC_{9-0.5-0.5}$ use even less cobalt and these are now being released and can be expected to be in widespread use by 2021/22.

Lithium Nickel Cobalt Aluminium Oxide NCA/Graphite offers a high energy density, a good power density and a long life but requires careful management to avoid thermal runaway. NCA is better suited to small cylindrical cells and is not suited to pouch type. NCA's power density is exploited to the full in the Tesla 'Ludicrous' and 'Insane' modes of rapid acceleration.

Both NMC and NCA cells use graphite anode and increasingly use a graphite-silicon anode to increase energy capacity. Silicon expands significantly more than graphite in use and hence initially small amounts only have been added in order to avoid electrode cracking, but the amount of silicon is increasing gradually.

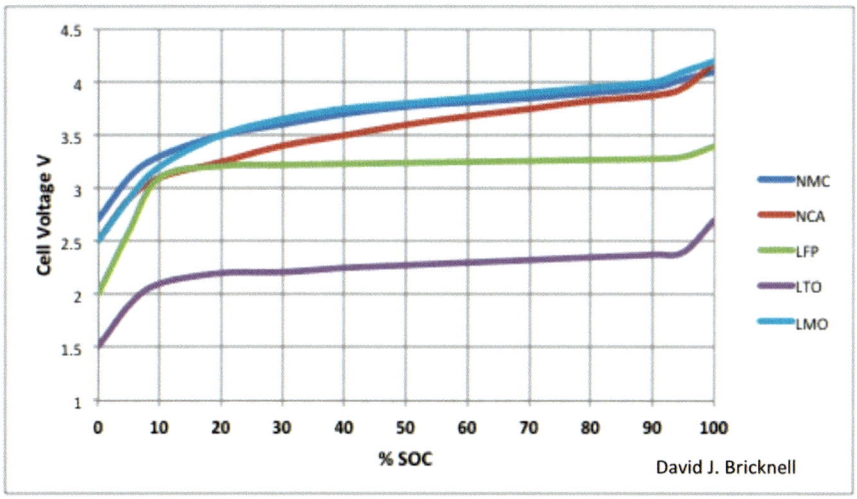

Illustrative voltage for cell discharge for various cell chemistries.
(NMC, NCA and LMO taken from AVT-INL testing. LTO and LFP from The Battery University.)

Future LIB developments

Cost, size and recharging time are three of the key areas for battery development.

- Cost can be reduced by scale and also by reducing high-cost minerals, such as Cobalt;

- Size by improving energy density - storing more energy in a given space; and

- Recharging time by improving electrode chemistry to accept charge quicker.

Using **Silicon** together with graphite in the anode significantly improves battery capacity/energy density. Silicon absorbs charge differently from graphite and so designing the battery to cope with the electrode delamination has proved difficult but increasing amounts of silicon are now being integrated into LIBs. [70]

Most BEV manufacturers are concentrating on two types of batteries – Tesla with NCA (in cylindrical cells) and most others on Nickel-Rich NMC (in pouch cells).

Tesla's near-term development will involve improved cell chemistry by increasing the amount of silicon into the graphite anode in order to increase energy density. Tesla expects to increase energy density by about 5% each year. [71]

The NMC users have moved from LMO-NMC to NMC_{111}, meaning equal amounts of nickel, manganese and cobalt. Cobalt is by far the most expensive of the constituents for the cathode – it is about 5 times more than nickel and 30 times more than manganese. In order to reduce costs but also to improve performance, the next step was NMC_{622} and NMC_{721}, and then to NMC_{811} (80% nickel, 10% manganese and 10% cobalt) [72] and even $NMC_{9-0.5-0.5}$ [73].

LG Chem and SK Innovation are now bringing NMC_{811} to market in 2020. Samsung SDI have indicated 2021 for BMW cars.

Samsung/BMW show their next step (5-years) as NMC_{811} with silicon/graphite anode and then in around 10-years as 'all solid state' electrolyte – each step reducing costs and further improving energy density.

LG Chem are reported to be developing NMCA with added aluminium and reduced cobalt with up to 90% Nickel for around 2022 timescale [74]. Other manufacturers, such as SVOLT, are pursuing similar developments. [75]

Other longer-term developments include:

Zinc-Air – better known for hearing aids but has the potential as an BEV battery [76].

Lithium-Sulphur – a potentially low cost and temperature-tolerant cell but one that has yet to be successfully developed [77].

Lithium-Air –offering potentially 5-10 times the energy density of today's batteries but is at the beginning of its development [78].

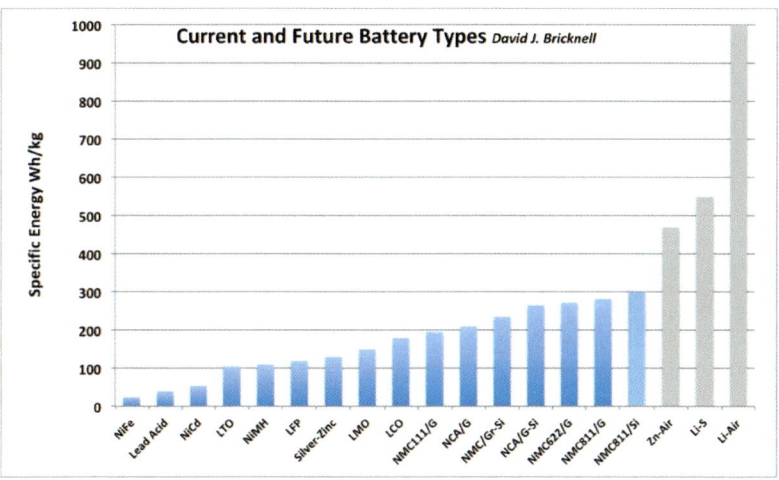

One significant development eagerly anticipated for some time is the solid-state LIB where the liquid electrolyte is replaced with a solid ceramic electrolyte. Solid State LIBS will be more energy dense, maybe two to three times higher [79].

A key characteristic is the lack of an SEI so charging rates can be higher and cycle life longer. Seeo/Bosch, Dyson/Sakti, Fisker, Toyota, VW/Quantumscape and BMW/Solid Power are all working to commercialise solid-state batteries by the early 2020s. [80]

Tesla look to be addressing solid state with the acquisition of Maxwell. Maxwell are known for supercapacitors but have been developing dry electrode/solid state Li-Ion cells offering 300W/kg with a path to 500kW/kg with a 90% capacity retention after 1,500 cycles [81].

Battery Life and Degradation

For a BEV, **Battery Life** is considered to be when its **State of Health** is either 80% (or 70%, for some manufacturers). State of Health refers to the **battery capacity** now compared with capacity new.

Battery Life is a combination of **Calendar life** or time including at rest and **Cycle life** or usage including charging and discharging.

Battery Capacity reduces due to **Battery Degradation** [82]. Degradation occurs **when:**

- there is a loss of active sites for lithium ions on the anode and on the cathode.
- there is a loss in the amount of lithium ions that are cyclable between the anode and cathode current collectors.
- there is an increase in electrical resistance through the thickening of the SEI and cathode surface films or through the disruption of the anode or cathode internal structure preventing ions from landing.

Degradation will manifest itself as a reduction in range and performance in two ways:

- **Capacity loss:** - the battery is permanently unable to store as much energy, so your range is reduced;
- **Resistance rise:** - the charge and/or discharge rate is permanently lower. Additional heat will be generated when doing either of these, so efficiency is further reduced meaning energy consumption is up and because energy consumption is up, range is reduced. Maximum power may be also reduced if the higher cell resistance results in higher cell temperatures.

Capacity loss and resistance rise are in turn are influenced by high and low cell temperature, by high and low States of Charge SOC, and by high charge and discharge rates.

It will be beneficial to maximising battery life to avoid:

- parking for long times at high temperatures
- aggressive use at low temperatures,
- parking for long times at high SOC,
- extended use at low SOC,
- repeated aggressive driving
- repeated rapid charging.

The **Battery Management System** will manage many of the things that will affect your battery life and prevent the car going into danger zones, but the driver can also contribute to prolonging battery life by avoiding or minimising the driver-controlled factors above.

Calendar Life is, as it suggests, directly related to the time since the cell was manufactured. Cell capacity will decrease as time elapses because the SEI will thicken over time due to deposits of active Lithium. From the moment the cell is first manufactured, the SEI forms and protects the graphite electrode from the electrolyte – this causes an initial loss of capacity until the cell stabilises. The SEI continues to thicken over time continuing the loss of capacity in a broadly linear manner until the cell reaches a rapid deterioration phase. Cells will age more quickly over time if kept at higher temperatures and conversely will age more slowly if kept very cold.

Cycle Life is the number of complete charge and discharge cycles the battery can sustain before its nominal 80% capacity is exceeded. One cycle is a complete charge and discharge. Five partial 20% charge and discharges are equal to one cycle.

Battery capacity will reduce with increasing number of cycles due to increased cell resistance. This will be exacerbated with:

- **higher cell voltages (higher SOC),** even if only achieved briefly. This is due to decomposition of the electrolyte, SEI and binder; dendrite formation on the cathode; and graphite exfoliation on the anode.

- **Low cell voltage (low SOC)** even if only achieved briefly. Very low states of charge cause the copper of the anode and aluminium of the cathode to dissolve and then to form dendrites

- **higher charge and discharge rates** will increase the loss of lithium to the SEI layer (except LTO). This loss occurs due to, particle cracking where parts of the anode are prevented from receiving or sending ions due to the crack, cyclable ions are used to remake the SEI on the crack face, and the SEI itself decomposes and recomposes using more cyclable lithium), a loss of electrical contact with the binder, and structural disordering.

- **high rates of charging and discharging at very low cell temperatures**. Lithium plating will occur at very at low temperatures - the charge rates force ion transfer at a rate faster than a cold anode can accept them. This will manifest itself as spiky dendrites causing a loss of active lithium and the potential for catastrophic puncturing of the separator potentially leading to short circuit and thermal runaway.

- **higher Depth of Discharge (DOD).** Anode and cathode will expand during charging and discharging, typically by up to 13% which can lead to loss of electrical contact and this is exacerbated by the speed of charge/discharge and by lower temperature. Smaller Depth of Discharge DoD is better for life than larger DoD and the expansion is lower and slower – so ABC (Always Be Charging) is still a good strategy. There is no advantage to waiting!

- Operation at **high temperatures can** cause binder dissolution between the particle and the current collector, and a thickening of the cathode surface film. These cause an increase in electrical resistance. At high temperatures and SOC, the cathode will also suffer from dissolution into the electrolyte – Manganese is particularly susceptible to this.

The Rate of Charge and of Discharge (C-Rate) and Depth of Discharge affect battery life as the processes that take place during discharge will be less complete the more rapidly it occurs.

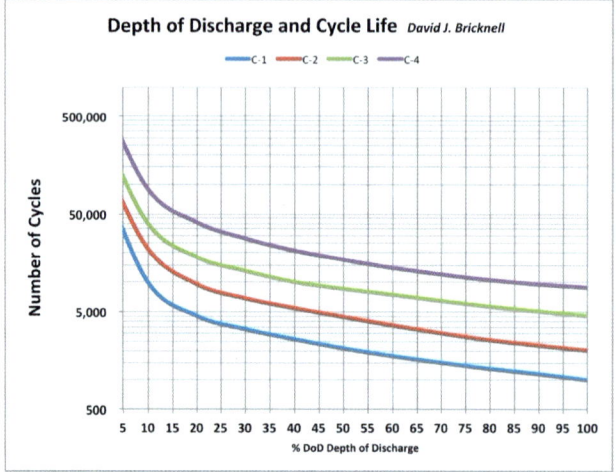

Chart showing the typical relationship between Depth of Discharge and number of cycles for different rates of discharge C-Rate.

The 'Million-Mile' Battery

For the same BEV, the DOD per cell is lower on larger capacity battery packs for the same journey. For the 20kWh ~ 80-mile range per charge, 1,000 full cycles correspond to 80,000 – 118,000 miles which at an average 10,000 to 12,000 miles per annum equates to about eight years.

For a 60kWh 240mile battery pack, the same annual mileage is only a third of the cycle life, albeit the larger battery capacity may well encourage longer and faster road trips incurring higher-C-rates and probably higher DODs.

To achieve a 'million-mile battery' with a life of 1250cycles in a BEV at 4miles/kWh requires a battery of 200kWh – the capacity of the eagerly anticipated Tesla Roadster. For a BEV with a battery of 100kWh will require a cycle life of 2500.

Cell Voltage and Cell Capacity

As the cell discharges the voltage reduces from its maximum until it reaches the minimum operating voltage. The maximum for today's LIB is usually between 4.1 and 4.2V and the minimum around 3.0-3.5V depending on the manufacturer's strategy for cell life protection: the minimum operating voltage being above the minimum cell voltage - the rather steep reduction in cell voltage that can be seen in the chart below as the cell nears complete discharge will require reduced discharging rates at such low voltages.

As the cell ages and as cycling reduces its capacity the shape of the discharge curve remains the same, but the Capacity Ah reduces, as can be seen in the graph below

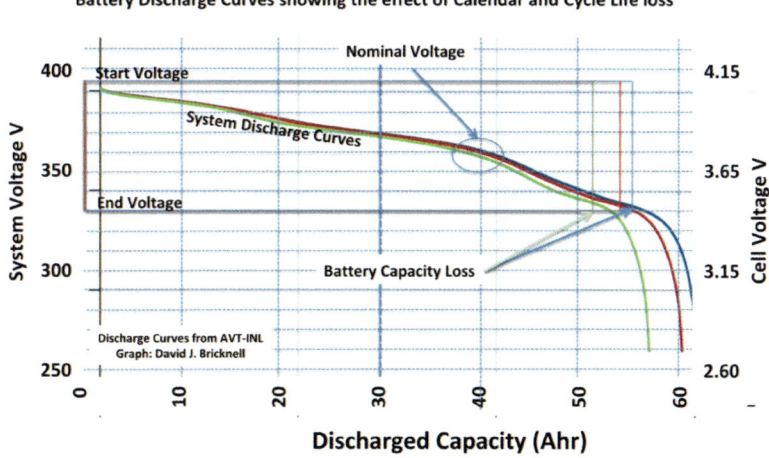

Battery Discharge Curves showing the effect of Calendar and Cycle Life loss

Ion transfers within the battery cell are affected by **cell voltage** and **battery temperature**:

Cell Voltage - Once all the available Ion transfers within a cell have been completed and it has reached its upper cell voltage, then forcing more energy into a cell will cause it to heat up whilst producing irreversible chemical reactions that will damage the cell. Similar irreversible reactions occur when discharging the cell below its lower voltage limit.

Temperature of Operation

The hotter the battery, the faster the ion transfers will be. Higher temperatures will mean higher power and higher capacity but also a shorter life. [83]

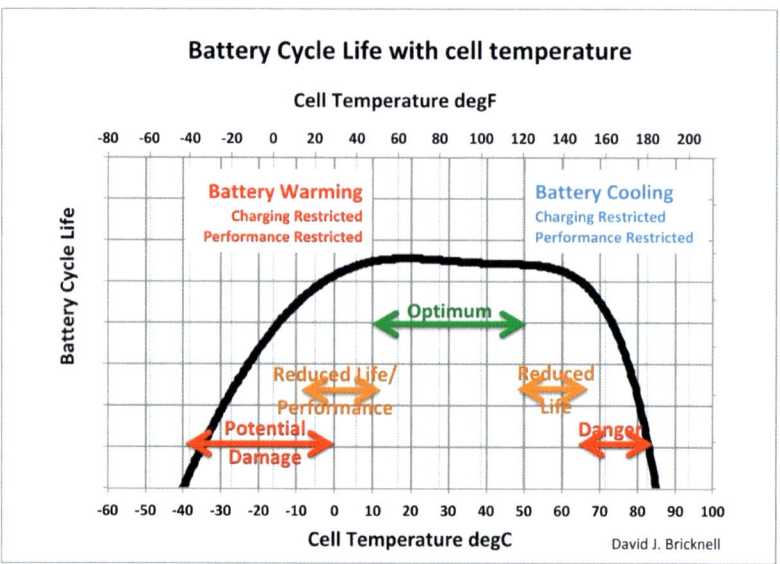

Batteries have an optimum operating temperature. Operating outside of this can lead to reduced cycle life and to performance degradation.

As an illustration of the battery cell temperature strategies deployed by BEV suppliers:

Where applied, battery preconditioning generally brings the battery cell temperatures to 10°C (50°F) – there is some range benefits to this but preserving battery cycle life is the biggest benefit.

Regeneration is generally restricted below 10°C (50°F). Tesla prevents regeneration below zero C (32°F), other manufacturers will have similar battery strategies.

Rapid charging of cells exceeding 50°C (120°F) is normally prevented.

Battery usable capacity varies with cell temperature and discharge rate

As the battery cell temperature drops, due to reduced ambient temperature, the usable battery capacity reduces. This means that some of the energy charged into the battery cannot be accessed.

This chart shows the reduction in cell capacity (at a 1-C discharge rate) with reducing cell temperature for a generic NMC LIB.

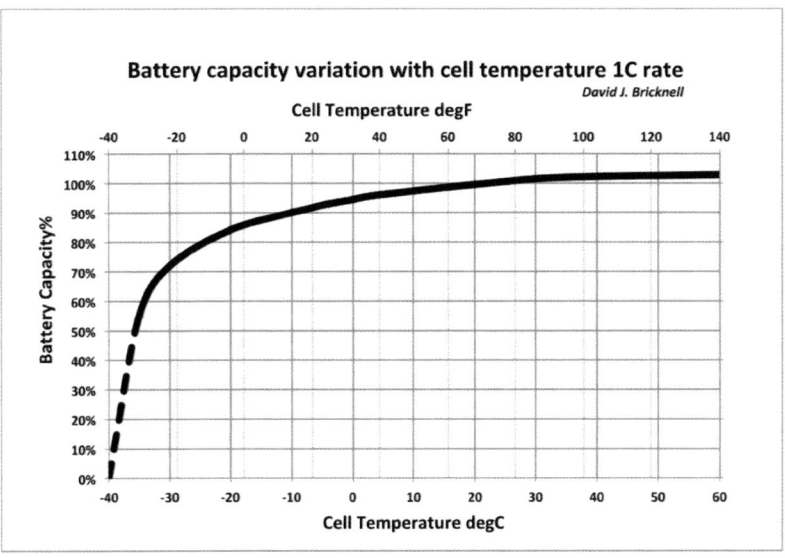

BEVs generally offer three strategies for protecting against the impact of lower cell temperatures

- preconditioning of the battery to about 10°C/50F.

- power restriction, reducing the available discharge rate (power and acceleration).

- Charging rate restriction / battery cell heating

Discharge/Charge Rate C-Rate

The battery C-Rate is a term expressing how quickly the battery is discharging energy compared to the total battery capacity per hour.

Lithium-Ion cells show a reduction in cell voltage as the cells discharge. The rate at which the cell voltage reduces is affected by the rate at which the discharge occurs – higher rates of power will more rapidly reduce the cell voltage in turn reducing the capacity of the cell.

Similarly, higher charge rates will more quickly increase cell voltage – one of the reasons for slowing charge rate when nearing high SOC.

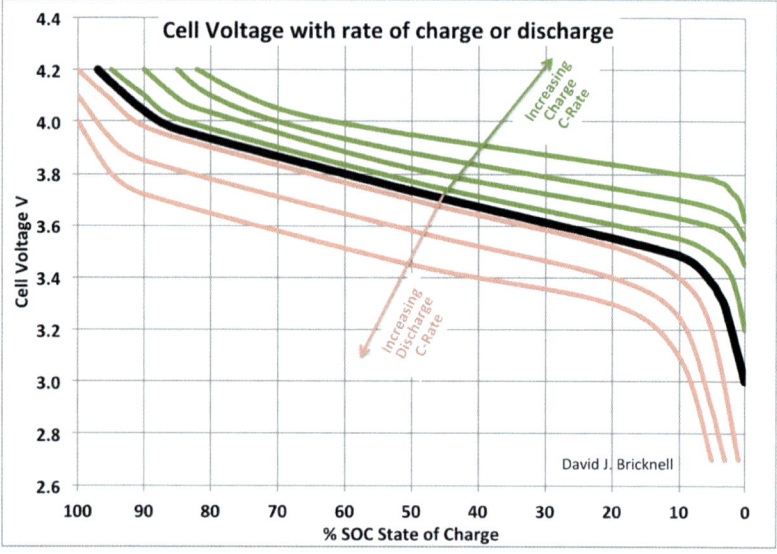

Cell and System Voltage in operation

Cell and System Voltage will vary considerable over the driving cycle depending upon the nature of the drive – urban, highway/motorway and whether the drive is aggressive in nature or not.

The chart below shows a typical BEV (NMC battery) driven over a variety of standard driving cycles including an aggressive cycle. This chart shows the drive at a cold -4°C/25°F and demonstrates the wide divergence from a smooth static capacity discharge. In this case the BMS has a set system 395V / cell 4.1V upper and 330V / 3.4V lower limit

During operation, particularly under acceleration, the instantaneous cell voltage will drop below 3.4V - during a similar test at -4°C the cell voltage can be seen as instantaneously low as 3.23V (system 310V) and during similar tests at -17°C cell voltages as low as 2.9V (system 280V) can be seen.

The car's management system will seek to avoid the cell voltage dropping too low and will restrict power if such an event seems likely.

Driving Cycle at -4°C - Energy discharged over driving cycles 17.47kWhrs

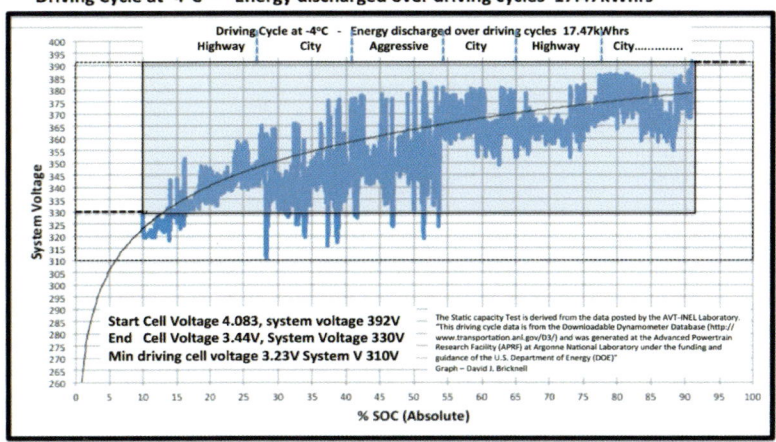

Usable battery capacity is less than the absolute capacity. The BMS does not allow operation into the no-go areas and the top and bottom of the battery capacity. Manufacturers take a different view on the reserved SOC top and bottom. BMW keeps around 10% at either end with a further 5% reserved at the bottom for restricted driving. Tesla use a range of around 6% to 95% [84]

Usable Battery Capacity

BEV manufacturers take different views on the usable capacity compared to absolute capacity and set their upper and lower SOC differently depending upon cell composition, BMS, and cooling and heating system.

Shown in the illustration below is the absolute and usable limits for a BMW Prismatic Cell BEV. The top 10% and bottom 10% (approximately) provide the safety reserve for operation together with a reduced performance band for additional safety and range.

Tesla operates a similar band with around ~6% at the bottom and ~95% at the top – battery size and model will influence both limits.

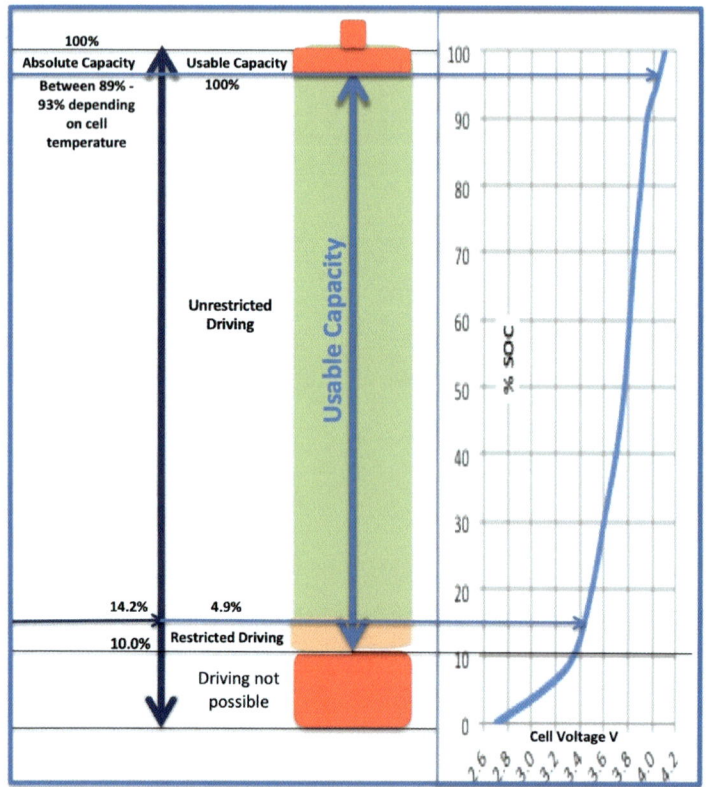

BMW i3 Prismatic Cell absolute and Usable SOC together with cell voltage as measured by Argonne.[85]

Usable Capacity will vary with a combination of cell temperature and discharge rate.

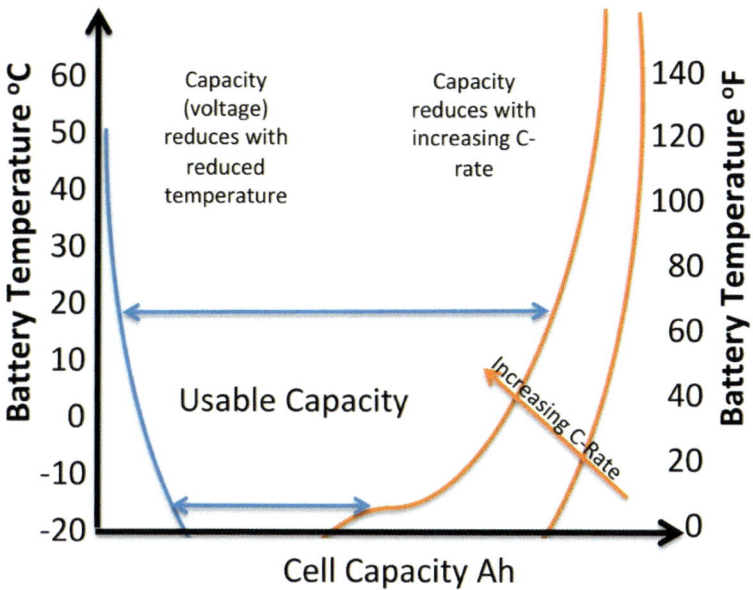

For the BEV LIB the above graph illustrates the 'full' battery reducing as cell temperature falls – around 10% loss from 30°C to 0°C. More dramatic is the effect of discharge rate at lower temperatures where high discharge rates (rapid acceleration and high speeds) will reduce the effective battery capacity substantially due to rapid internal cell heating.

Battery Formats

Three shapes of LIBs – cylindrical, prismatic and pouch. All configurations are used in different manufacturers BEVs with each having their own strengths:

Cylindrical - The cylindrical battery is like a Swiss-roll or jelly-roll of positive electrode (normally a copper foil base), separator, negative electrode (normally an aluminium foil base) and separator rolled up. Anode and Cathode materials are coated onto the metal foils.

Tesla is the principal BEV proponent of cylindrical cells although the configuration has widespread usage outside of BEVs. Most popular cylindrical size is the 18650 as used in the S&X (18mm in diameter and 65mm in length) and now the 2170 (21mm in diameter and 70mm in length). At the battery day in September 2020, Tesla stated their intention to move to a larger 4680 tabless cylindrical cell offering five times more energy per cell, 16% more range, six times more power and reduce cost per kWh by 14%. [86]

Cylindrical cells do seem to offer very high packing densities and, because of the small cell energy and large numbers of cells, offer greater flexibility to vary battery pack capacity.

The Tesla Model S 100D uses 8,256 of the 18650 format NCA cells in its battery pack for about 100kWh. Photo courtesy of Oleg Alexandrov (cc-by-sa-3.0).

Tesla's Model 3 Long Range uses 4416 of the 2170 cells for about 80kWh. The 2170 offers about 50% more available volume than the 18650.

Photo courtesy of jzh2074 (cc-by-sa-4.0).

Prismatic cells use layers of anode, separator, cathode, separator, etc., within a hard, aluminium case. The electrodes and separators are wound, as a flattened spiral, or stacked as sheets giving a lower density pack size than the cylindrical arrangement.

Significantly less cells are normally used in prismatic battery packs compared to cylindrical or pouch as the cell Amp-hours can be much greater e.g. Samsung SDI has 26, 28, 60, 94, and 120Ah available.

BMW are the only user of this cell format. Whether a further increase in cell amp-hours is coming or whether BMW will now choose two or more smaller cells in parallel with 96 in series is not currently known. [87]

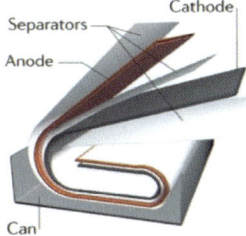

Typical construction of a prismatic battery cell.

Samsung SDI Prismatic NMC cells within an i3 module package. Photo courtesy of Gonville Bromhead

Pouch, used by Jaguar, Nissan, Renault, GM, VW, Hyundai, Mercedes, Audi and others allows a very flat and thin installation. The electrodes are bonded together with a polymer that also acts as the separator. The electrolyte is infused into the polymer and becomes a gel meaning that the battery can be packaged in a foil envelope instead of a solid case.

The foil envelopes are then packed into a module and the modules stacked within the overall battery pack. Pouch cells are also known as LiPo or Lithium Polymer. Minimal cell packaging should lead to a higher energy density although some structure is essential to contain and constrain the pouches.

Pouches tend to be large slim and envelope-shaped which can present a large surface area for cooling. Pouches can be stacked flat or on edge, those on edge are tending towards very wide and very short, almost a strip-like letter-box format, minimizing cabin intrusion.

Wide format LG Chem NMC Cell and the packaging within the Jaguar I-Pace battery pack. Jaguar has 36 modules per pack with 12 cells per module.

I-Pace picture courtesy of Halit Murat Gültekin

Pack configurations

Within the battery pack the cells can be connected in series, in parallel or in a combination of both.

Serial connection determines the battery pack voltage – add the voltages of each cell in series together.

Parallel connection adds the current of the batteries together but holds to the cell voltage – add the Ah of each cell in parallel together.

Battery Capacity is pack voltage V multiplied by battery Ah.

BEV manufacturers use various combinations of serial and parallel configurations.

EV	Manufacturer Grouping	Cell	Format	Parallel	Series	No. of cells	Cell Voltage Nominal V	Cell Capacity Ah	System Voltage Max	kWh (Usable) Est.	AC Recharge Energy EPA kWh
BMW i3 60Ah	BMW	Samsung SDI	Prismatic	1	96	96	3.70	60.0	400	18.8	21.7
BMW i3 94Ah				1	96	96	3.68	94.0	400	27.2	32.3
BMW i3 120Ah				1	96	96	3.70	120.0	400	37.9	45.1
Mini Electric				1	96	96	3.68	94.0	400	27.2	34.3
Smart EQ	Daimler Benz		Pouch	3	92	276	3.65	16.9	383	16.7	21.4
GM Bolt/Ampera-E	GM	LG Chem	Pouch	3	96	288	3.65	62.8	400	65.0	73.6
Hyundai Ioniq	Hyundai Motor Group	LG Chem	Pouch	1	96	96	3.75	78.0	400	25.5	29.5
Hyundai Ioniq				1	88	88	3.63	120.0	400	35.5	42.8
Hyundai Kona 39				2	90	180	3.63	60.0	400	36.5	42.8
Hyundai Kona 64				3	98	294	3.63	60.0	408	64.0	71.3
Kia Soul		SK Innovation		2	100	200	3.60	40.0	417	28.0	34.1
Kia Soul 64				3	98	294	3.63	60.0	400	60.0	
Kia e-Niro				3	98	294	3.63	60.0	400	60.0	70.9
Jaguar i-Pace	JLR	LG-Chem	Pouch	4	108	432	3.59	58.0	450	84.7	104.0
i-Miev		Lithium Energy	Prismatic	1	88	88	3.7	50.0	367	14.2	17.9
Nissan Leaf 20	Renault-Nissan-Mitsubishi	AESC	Pouch	2	96	192	3.65	33.0	400	20.0	24.6
Nissan Leaf 40				2	96	192	3.65	57.5	400	37.0	44.8
Nissan Leaf e+				3	96	288	3.70	57.5	400	57.0	68.4
Renault Zoe 20		LG Chem		2	96	192	3.75	36.0	400	22.8	
Renault Zoe 40				2	96	192	3.75	65.0	400	41.0	
Renault Zoe 50				2	96	192	3.75	78.0	400	52.0	
Tesla S 8S (pre2015)	Tesla	Tesla-Panasonic	Cylindrical	74	96	7104	3.65	3.1	400	73.4	95.5
Tesla S 8S (2015)				74	96	7104	3.65	3.3	400	73.4	91.1
Tesla S 90D (2017)				70	96	6720	3.65	3.4	400	78.0	96.4
Tesla S/X 75 SR				64	96	6144	3.65	3.4	400	71.6	84.6
Tesla S/X 100 LR				86	96	8256	3.65	3.4	400	95.7	111.7
Tesla 3 SR +				32	96	3072	3.65	5.0	400	52.0	62.0
Tesla 3 LR				46	96	4416	3.65	5.0	400	75.0	89.4
Audi E-Tron 55	VAG	LG Chem	Pouch	4	108	432	3.68	60.0	450	84.2	96.5
Porsche Taycan				2	198	396	3.66	64.5	850	84.0	98.1
VW e-Golf		Panasonic		3	88	264	3.67	37.0	367	30.0	36.3

BEV manufacturers tend to package their cells into a number of modules before assembling them into the overall pack. Tesla, in their 3 and Y, take a different approach. They use four large packs into which cells are installed on a bandolero to fill the pack – all cells are installed the same way up. [88]

System series and parallel configurations are then arranged by a metal 'Christmas-tree' type arrangement across the individual cells. Should the pack need to adopt 800V the rearrangement is relatively simple.

Clearly the building blocks of each cell will impact on the configuration of the battery pack. Most BEVs use 96 cells in series but different numbers in parallel. Hyundai/Kia have extended the number in series to 98 and 100 and the I-Pace and E-Tron both use 108. Using 96 cells leads to pack voltage of approximately a nominal 350V and max 400 whilst 108 means 388-397V nominal and 450V max.

The i3 uses all cells in series in order to reach the required system voltage. Nissan's Leaf, with cells of just over half the energy (Ah) of the i3, reaches system voltage with the same number of cells but needs twice as many in order to provide the required system energy. GM's Bolt uses three times as many cells of similar energy to the i3 in order to achieve a battery pack three times the capacity and the Jaguar i-Pace uses four times.

Tesla use the 18650 (S&X) and 2170 (3&Y) cylindrical cells; it needs 96 cells in series to reach system voltage and, for the S85, 74 in parallel to reach battery energy capacity (74p, 96s) and for the S100 it needs 86 in parallel (86p, 96s). The more circuits in parallel, the more modular the battery pack can be whilst holding to a common system voltage. Model 3 uses a 400V system with the LR having 46p, 96s arrangement and the SR+ having an estimated 32p, 96s arrangement.

An 800V system will have twice the number of cells in series – the first car with an 800V system is the Porsche Taycan. This will allow a lighter installation with thinner wires as, with double the voltage, the same power can be achieved with half the current. Charging may be a little quicker due to less waste heat being developed. [89]

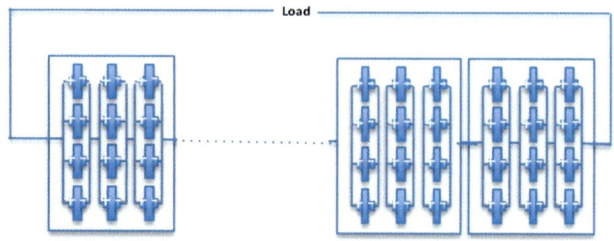

Parallel connection of multiple series connected battery cells is required when the current available from individual cells is insufficient for the required power or series connecting more than 96-108 cells would lead to too high a system voltage.

Battery Temperature Management

Different cell chemistries will have differing operational temperatures.

For the mixed-metal-graphite cells (LFP, LMO, NMC and NCA) an operational cell temperature range of -40°C to +50°C (-40°F to 120°F) is typical – not ambient temperature but cell temperature, cells being slower to respond to ambient temperature changes.

However, at cell temperatures below zeroC (32F) the significant increase in cell internal resistance will reduce the performance of mixed metal–graphite LIBs on discharge rate in order to avoid excessive internal heating. Manufacturers will prevent charging until cells have been heated to above zeroC in order to avoid lithium plating on the anode leading to reduced battery cycle life. The optimum cell temperature for performance is 25°C to 40°C and for life 10-20 °C.

BEVs have adopted different cooling strategies broadly depending upon cell type.

BEVs that share a platform with an ICE all use Pouch Cells and are cooled by forced air. This is the simplest arrangement and is or was adopted by the Hyundai Ioniq, early Kia Soul and the VW e-Golf. The battery pack is force air cooled by fan with ambient air. Hyundai and Kia have linked their system to the cooling or heating of cabin air in order to improve its performance. Renault's Zoe uses a similar system.

Nissan's Leaf used a very simple passive air cooling for its pouch cells which in hotter climates has not proved very successful. [90]

Other BEVs that use Pouch cells adopt a bottom cooling plate fed by a water glycol coolant that is either in combination with the motor and power electronics cooling circuit or is a discrete system with its own radiator. Some BEV models in some countries integrate the battery glycol cooling system with a refrigeration circuit and heat exchanger. GMs Bolt/Ampera-E, Jaguar I-Pace, Audi E-Tron, Porsche Taycan, Hyundai Kona, Kia e-Niro and latest Kia Soul all adopt variations of this arrangement which is suited to letterbox configuration vertically stacked pouch cell arrangements. Heating can be introduced into the coolant circuit either powered by resistive elements or a heat pump. [91] [92] [93]

BMW are the only manufacturer to have adopted large format prismatic cells. These cells have a high thermal mass and are quite slow to heat and cool. The prismatic cells are cooled by a refrigerant in evaporator tubes running underneath the prismatic cell modules. Contained within the battery-pack is the refrigerant cooling system sharing the same compressor as the air conditioning system. A battery pack resistive heater of (approx1kW) is fitted to pre-condition the battery pack during spells of cold weather. The pre-conditioning warms the battery cells to about 10°C / 50°F in order to minimize cycle-life loss and to allow recuperation of energy.

BMW i3 battery pack casing showing the evaporator cooling tubes running along the bottom of the casing. **Photo courtesy Philip Ivanier**

Tesla's Cylindrical Cells are cooled by water glycol coolant circulated between the rows of cells. A refrigerant/chiller is also integrated to reduce liquid coolant temperature as necessary and in the Tesla S&X an in-line heating element raises cell temperature when required. In addition, cell heating is implemented by activating the motor at zero rpm drawing power from the cells and hence self-heating the cell from the inside.

Cell heating can also be done by causing the cells to self-heat – Two small pieces of nickel foil are added into the cell jelly roll and these are connected in such a manner that cell heating occurs from the inside and not from the outside and hence heating is very rapid using a very small amount of energy to do so.

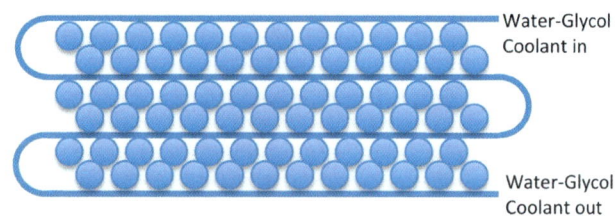

Water-Glycol Coolant in

Water-Glycol Coolant out

Cooling arrangement for the Tesla S & X. Cooling tubes are rather long for maintaining an even temperature for all cells in a module.

The Tesla 3 and Y have adopted a similar cell cooling arrangement but have refined the system in order to shorten cooling tubes to improve cooling performance for all the pack not just the first half on the circuit. Cooling tubes are tall and flat to ensure that the full height of the cell is cooled.

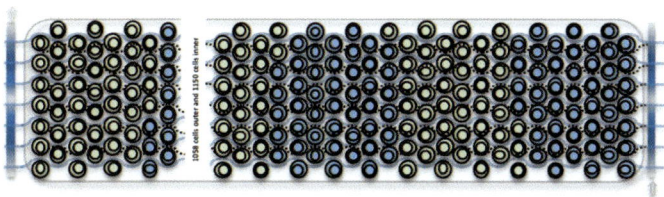

Manifold cooling arrangement for one of the modules of the TM3&Y. This arrangement has much improved efficiency of heat transfer than the older S&X design. Cells are installed already glued to a 'bandolero' within the module sandwiched between the cooling tubes. Each tube has a flat profile, is full height to the cylindrical cell, and has approximately 30 cooling tubes running through it to ensure effective cooling to the full height of all cells.

Preconditioning of battery

Low battery cell temperatures reduce available capacity and available power, will limit energy regeneration, impact on battery life, and will increase recharge time.

Preconditioning or heating of battery is done slowly to ensure that cells are warmed evenly and don't distort. The aim of preconditioning is to bring the battery to a temperature of about 10°C / 50°F.

A graph of the preconditioning process shows packets of heating being applied and this then being allowed to soak through before the next heating input. LIBs have a high thermal mass and are slow to warm and to cool; too much heat too quickly will lead to physical cell distortion.

This chart is for the BMW i3 but other BEVs use similar principle with different amounts of energy at different times.

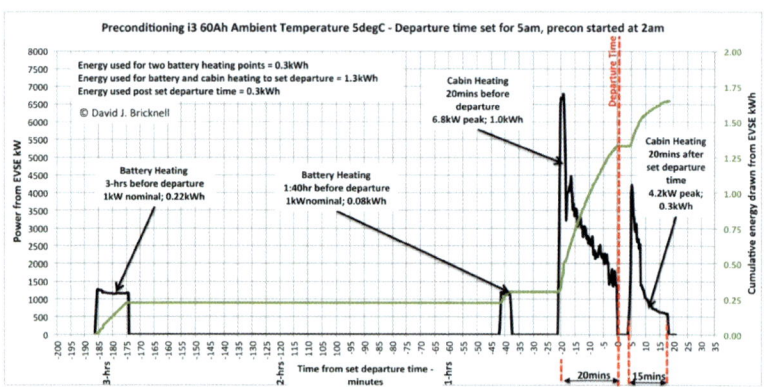

Typical preconditioning power and energy usage showing the early discrete packages of energy applied to heat the battery and then to let it soak through.

Tesla suggests preconditioning the battery for about an hour in very cold climates whilst plugged in. "When temperatures are near freezing, preconditioning will also heat your battery for better driving and charging performance. It is recommended to plug in to reduce range loss and start pre-conditioning about an hour before leaving since it can take some time to warm up the battery in colder weather"[94].

Battery Management System

The BMS has a key safety role in ensuring that the maximum cell voltage does not exceed the level where thermal runaway might occur; this can be as little as a few hundred millivolts over the maximum. Overvoltage, even by a little, can also significantly affect cell degradation and critically shorten battery life.

The BMS ensures that a uniform charge is provided to the HV battery. It measures the:

- system voltage,
- current flowing into or out from,
- individual cell voltages and temperatures, and
- calculates the State of Charge (SOC) and
- calculates the State of Health (SOH).

During charging, the BMS signals the cell voltage and temperature, (typically every tenth of a second), and, taking this into account, it demands the right level of current to be delivered by the charger.

The CSSU monitors every battery cell for cell voltage and temperature (cells differ due to manufacturing tolerances and ageing) and communicates with the BMS to adjust the charging and balance the cells for optimum performance.

Lithium Ion batteries typically have a nominal cell voltage of 3.6 to 3.75V and a maximum cell voltage of between 4.1 and 4.2V. Connecting 96 cells in series gives a nominal system voltage of 345 - 360v and a maximum of approximately 400V.

The BMS will also protect against over-discharge, the point where all lithium ions are removed from the graphite anode. This would lead to excessive corrosion and prevent further operation of the cell.

The State of Charge for a BEV is the actual calculated battery capacity at that moment compared to the maximum usable battery capacity: battery capacity for a LIB varies with cell temperature, the rate of charge and discharge, and the time between charges.

Measuring a battery's SOC to a specific accuracy (current to an accuracy of ±0.5% and voltage to an accuracy of better than ±0.1%) necessary for a BEV is quite difficult. BEV batteries are normally sampled by the BMS between 20 and 100 times per second.

Battery Cell balancing

Ensuring that the cells in series (90, 96, 98, 108, etc.) are balanced in order to avoid overcharging individual cells and to maximise battery capacity is a challenge: cells at the beginning of life have normal manufacturing variation and through life the imbalance can worsen if not managed. [95] [96]

During charging, the strongest cell will reach full first, leaving the weakest short of charge whilst during discharge the weakest cell is then depleted first meaning the most charged cells are never fully discharged. The total battery capacity is therefore reduced - this will worsen if not addressed.

Two different strategies can be adopted to resolve battery cell imbalance and to increase battery pack life and capacity: one is passive balancing and the other active balancing, albeit there are variations on each type.

- Passive balancing reduces the energy in the most charged cell and dissipates it through a resistor allowing the other cells to catch up; it is only done whilst charging or resting but not during discharging.

- Active balancing takes the extra energy from the highest charged cells and transfers it to the cells least charged; it can be implemented during charging and discharging.

Most of today's BEVs adopt passive balancing as it is relatively simple, is inexpensive, and well suited to smaller battery packs. Active balancing, implemented during charge and discharge, is more complex, more expensive, but is better suited to larger battery packs where charging to full is likely to be less frequent and to PHEV batteries which are rarely fully charged.

Passive cell balancing Once the charging session is complete and the battery cell has settled, the BMS will dissipate the energy from the highest charged cells through a resistor as heat. The BMS will then either top up, burn down and so on until the battery pack is even or it will await the next charge and iterate in that manner.

Manufacturers either encourage you to charge to full which for BMW is 100% usable but 90% absolute, or for Tesla to 90%. In both cases, it is important to leave the vehicle plugged in after the car has stopped charging whilst it balances the cells. Some manufacturers recommend occasionally running the vehicle to 10% and then fully charging in order to calibrate the BMS. [97]

The gap between the usable and gross battery capacity is used for passive balancing the battery as well as for maintaining the life of the battery.

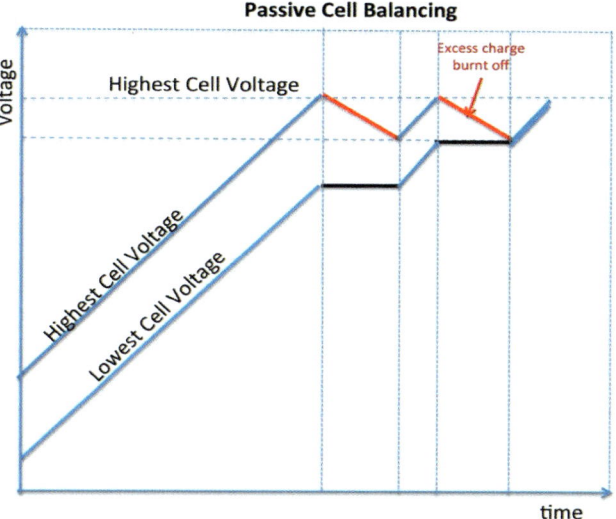

The chart above shows the principle of passive cell balancing. The cell with the highest voltage determines the point to stop charging. Once stopped the Cell Supervision Unit burns off the extra charge through a small resistor, hence the process may take some time after charging ends. With some Passive Systems, charging may restart and stop again to balance all the cells whilst others will use the next charge cycle, or preconditioning, to top up the cells again.

Active cell balancing uses either capacitive, inductive charge or, for faster balancing, power converter/PWM to distribute energy from the higher charged cells and provide it to the lower charged cells: this avoids the energy losses that are incurred by passive balancing.

Active balancing can be done whilst the cells are charging or discharging however the ability to balance is reduced as charge or discharge rate goes up, so if your BEV uses active balancing either drive more slowly occasionally or recharge on a lower powered charger every now and again.

Active balancing is well suited to larger battery packs and PHEV batteries and is preferable for energy reasons although the extra complexity comes at a cost.

This page left intentionally blank

Charging

Overview

Charging (and re-charging on-route or at a destination) is something new to drivers of CEV and, as with all newly introduced technologies, there are a myriad of different charging plugs, charging rates, charging companies and charging standards.

This section looks at the principles of charging, rates of charge and discharge, charging efficiency, the effects of charging on the battery (including heating and battery life), and State of Charge (SOC) (how it's measured and what it means) and the effects on charging speed of cell temperature.

National and International charging infrastructures are rapidly developing and expanding but for the moment there are many different charging companies and a multitude of different cost models – things will no doubt get clearer as the technology settles down.

The latest models of BEVs with larger capacity battery packs will mean, for some drivers, very little charging away from home, perhaps none at all for some. For the high-mileage traveller and for the once or twice a year vacation traveller, access to on-route rapid chargers is essential and here the power available at the charger is beginning to increase (50 to 150, 250 and on to 350kW) to cover the higher capacity battery packs, not forgetting, of course, that for many a rapid charge may entail only enough energy to complete the journey.

Many BEV drivers will have access to off-road home charging but not all. Those living in city centres may be in terrace houses and need to cross the pavement/sidewalk to plug in and some live-in apartments where their home electrical supply is not close to their parking spot. For some, charging their BEV can only be at a publicly available fast or rapid charging site.

BEV on a Mode 3 charger. Home charging, whilst not essential to BEV ownership, is the perfect solution for BEVs and is where around 80-90% of all battery charging is likely to be done.

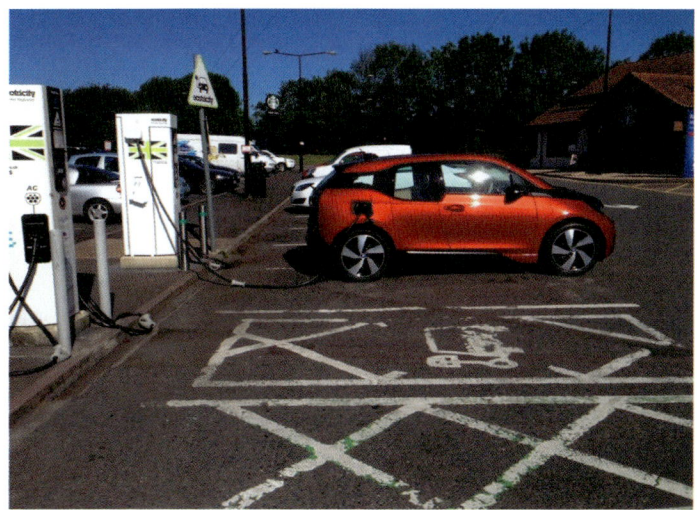

Mode 4 charging at an on-route CCS. Rapid chargers are essential for timely longer journeys.

Charging Li-Ion Batteries

The charging rate for Lithium Ion Batteries (LIBs) is dependent upon how quickly the ion transfers can take place within the cell.

These are temperature dependent with colder batteries requiring a longer time both to charge and to discharge:

- Too rapid a discharge can lead to cracking or crystal growth in the electrodes.

- Too rapid a charge will force too much current through the battery which can result in surplus ions being deposited irreversibly on the anode in the form of lithium metal (lithium plating).

BEVs carefully control the rate of charge and discharge. LIBs adopt a constant-current / constant-voltage charge system and hence any charging system must be able to monitor and control both current and voltage: LIBs can be damaged if the upper voltage limit is exceeded.

During the constant current CC phase, the charging current is at the maximum that the charger can provide, subject to any other maximum imposed by the manufacturer. Power will increase as voltage increases until the cell voltage nears its maximum after which the charger switches to a constant voltage CV mode. During the constant voltage phase, the current will initially decrease rapidly and then more gradually until, at a pre-determined point (typically <3% of rated current), full charge is reached when the charge is then abruptly stopped.

The current at the cut off will be dependent on the battery pack size: a 60kWh pack completing its charge at 3 times the current (same cell voltage) as that of a similar 20kWh pack.

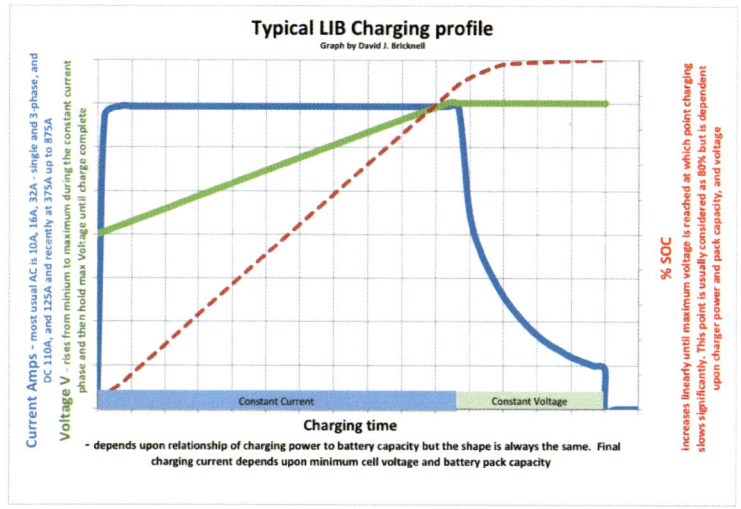

This chart shows a characteristic LIB charging profile. The actual charging time will depend on the charger power and the battery pack capacity and system voltage.

Charging Rate

Charging rate is important to the cycle life of the battery. Charging rate is expressed as C-Rate. This is the charging power related to the battery capacity – a 1-C rate for a 20kWh battery is 20kW and for a 60kWh battery is 60kW. As can be seen from the chart below up to 1.5-C is relatively benign and 2-C probably acceptable for occasional charging. Beyond 2-C the battery will deteriorate rapidly.

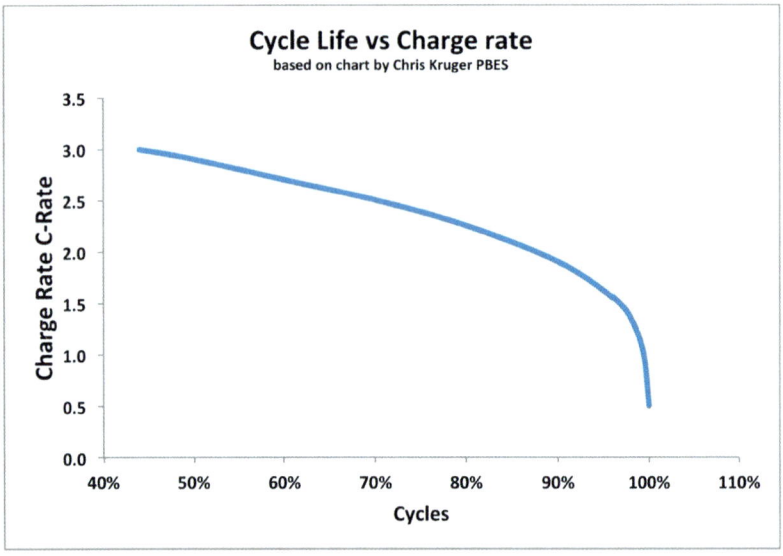

The Chart shows the deterioration in life from charging at higher C-rates (this is for LIBs with graphite anodes and excludes LTO and solid-state).

Today's 50kW rapid chargers are within 2-C for most of the current BEVs but as charger power increases to 150 then to 350kW the limitation of 2-C charge rate may not then result in quicker charges unless battery capacities increase significantly.

Charging Speeds

Charging speed is always noted as an issue for those new to BEVs but is much less of an issue for most experienced BEV drivers – availability and dependability being bigger issues.

Charge speed is often expressed as time from 10% to 80% State of Charge capacity but with such a large disparity of battery capacities, 20kWh to 100kWh, time to 80% is fairly meaningless.

The following table may help in understanding this. Charging speed is represented as a speed in range added per hour of charge (miles per hour or km per hour).

Charging Rates			
Power Amps/kW	Maximum Miles per hour	Maximum km per hour	notes
AC Single Phase			
10A/2.3kW	7-9	11-15	UK 3-pin plug
16A/3.6kW	12-15	19-24	Slow
20A/4.5kW	15-19	24-30	Typical lamppost
32A/7.4kW	24-30	40-48	Fast
AC Three Phase			
48A/11kW	33-45	50-70	i3, Zoe, TM3&Y
96A/22kW	66-90	105-145	Zoe, (TMS&X 16.5kW)
186A/43kW	130-170	210-275	early Zoe, no longer used
DC			
44kW-50kW	132-200	212-322	CCS & CHAdeMO
120kW-140kW	360-560	580-900	Tesla v2 Supercharger
250kW	750-1000	1200-1600	Tesla v3 Supercharger
100kW-350kW	300-1400	480-2250	CCS Ultra Chargers

Table showing the charging speed (miles/hour and km/hr) for the various charging connectors available in the UK today. All of these connector speeds have a role with BEVs albeit the 43kW connector is now only relevant ta one legacy car, no current BEVs use it. Only one current BEV uses 22kW with most 3-phase charging now at 11kW. One BEV can charge up to 16.5kW on a 22kW connection.

Both AC and DC charging have their place within a charging infrastructure.

Charging Modes

The BEV battery pack is always charged with Direct Current (DC) with the conversion from Alternating Current (AC) to DC being done either in the BEV or on the off-car charger. [98]

In Europe, the modes of charging for BEVs are defined in IEC 61851 and plugs, sockets, connectors and cable assemblies are defined in IEC 62196.

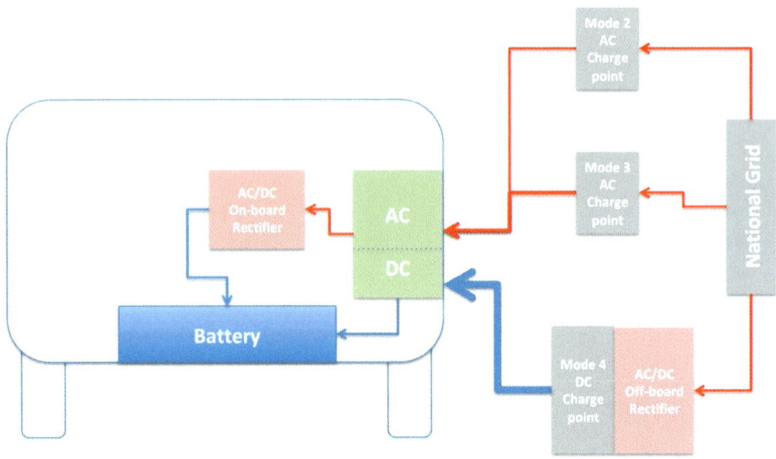

Illustration showing the various modes of charging a BEV. For Modes 2 and 3 the rectifier is on-board the vehicle; for Mode 4, the rectifiers are off-board.

In Modes 1, 2, and 3 the conversion from AC to DC is done within the vehicle. In Mode 4, the conversion of AC to DC is done in the off-car charging unit and bypasses the AC/DC rectifiers in the vehicle – this minimises both the size of the on-car AC/DC rectifiers (and their subsequent inefficiency at lower power) and the impact on the on-board vehicle's cooling system.

Mode 1 (up to 16A per phase) is not often used because of the lack of communication between the vehicle and the voltage supply. No current BEV uses this connection.

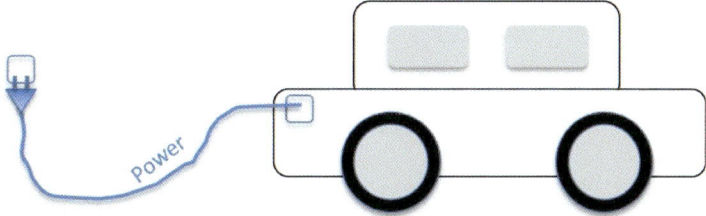

Mode 2 (up to 32A per phase) is used from a non-dedicated power supply such as a domestic power socket. The control and protection device is integrated into the charging cable and the AC-DC rectifier is in the vehicle. This cable is used for the slowest charges.

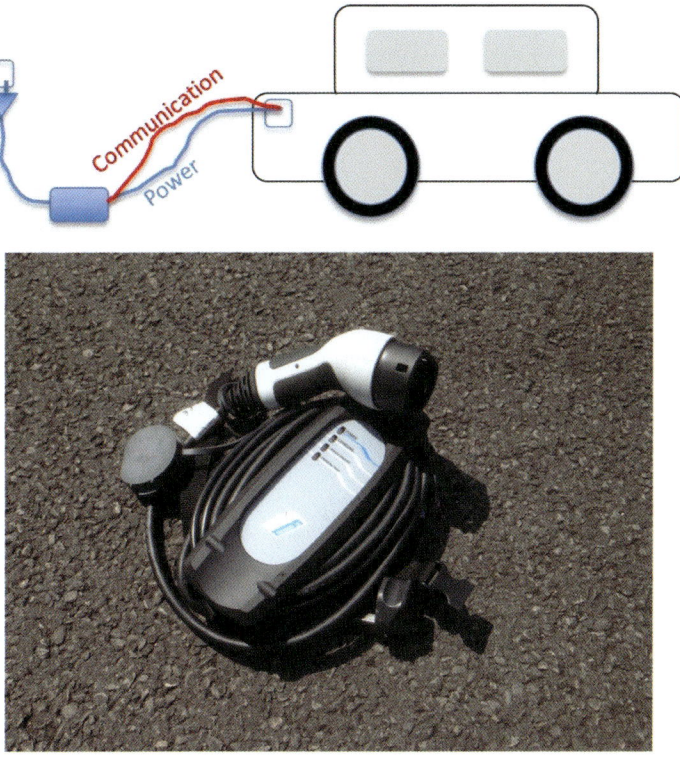

Mode 2 Charger for slow-speed charging

Mode 3 Either 230V 1-phase (up to 16kW/70A) or 400V 3-phase (up to 44kW/63A) supply is used from a dedicated EV charging station either installed at home or on route. The control, communication and protection functions are all integrated into the charge point with the charger device (AC-DC rectifier) being in the vehicle.

Most BEV drivers have a Mode 3 home/domestic charge point installed at 32A/7.4kW (230V).

Mode 3 dedicated EVSE

The charge cable can be separate or tethered to the EVSE as a user option.

For Mode 2 and 3, charging utilises on-board AC/DC rectifier(s); these are usually optimised around 16A and 32A single phase and 3-phase meaning 3.7kW, 7.4kW, and 11 kW and 22kW for 3-phase.

The GM Bolt/Ampera-E, VW e-Golf, Hyundai Ioniq and Kona, Kia e-Niro, Jaguar I-Pace and Nissan Leaf all include AC charging up to 32A.

The Tesla Model 3/Y and BMW i3 can both use either 32A/7.4kW single phase or use three on-board rectifiers thereby optimising for 16A,

32A single phase and 48A three phase; most other BEVs use single phase 32A/7.4kW.

The Renault Zoe and Kangoo make use of the powertrain inverter/rectifier to enable rapid charging at 43kW. The use of such a large rectifier leads to rather slow charging at lower power levels of the sort found domestically. Renault has now adopted the CCS Combo for high-power rapid charging.

The Tesla Model S latest model can charge at 16.5kW on three phase 22kW charger through three 5.5kW rectifiers (UK market). Previous Model S could charge at either 11 or 22kW. [99]

Mode 4 DC Charging. Mode 4 is a dedicated DC rapid charging from an external charger. Rapid charging EVSEs use AC electricity from the grid and convert it to DC in the charging unit before it gets to the vehicle.

Currently there are two competing open rapid charge systems available - CCS, and CHAdeMO, and one proprietary - Tesla Super Charger. There is also one used solely in China - GB/T 20234.3-2011 DC.

When the EVSE is connected to the BEV, the charger detects the connection and then signals to the BEV that the DC circuit has been made. The BEV's Battery Management System BMS responds with its charge level, battery voltage, and the current the battery can accept. Charging is managed by the external charger and is based on data communicated by the BEV.

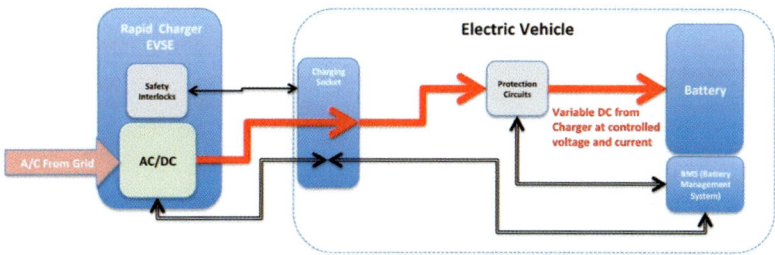

The BMS communicates with the Rapid Charger EVSE to control voltage and current during charging, constantly identifying the state of charge and monitoring all sensor signals of the high-voltage battery including temperature. In order to ensure optimal progress of the charging procedure, the BMS calculates current values for the maximum charging power based on these values and communicates these every tenth of a second.

The BMS controls heating/cooling of the high-voltage battery throughout the charging procedure. This contributes to a quick and efficient charging procedure. Safety functions for isolating the battery are also contained in the BMS.

Rapid and Ultra-Rapid charger hub in Falkirk illustrate the type of facilities necessary for both on-route and around town rapid charging. There must be sufficient chargers available to have a reasonable expectation of being able to charge on arrival or quite quickly thereafter.

CHAdeMO – (CHArge de MOve) developed by Nissan and Mitsubishi in 2010 (together with Tokyo Electric Power Company and Fuji Heavy Industries) with Toyota joining the standard later. CHAdeMO can deliver up to 50kW and 120A at up to 500V DC. CHAdeMO 1.2 enables 200kW (400A at 500V).[100]

A 400kW CHAdeMO 2.0 standard was announced in 2018 but has yet to be made available. This standard would deliver 400A at 1000V through a liquid cooled cable assembly. At 400V 160kW would be available.

A collaboration with China's GB/T has led to CHAdeMO 3.0, or ChaoJi, providing up to 500kW (600A at up to 1500V) [101].

CCS system – Combined Charging System developed by the majority of European and US car manufacturers and supported by SAE and ACEA with the aim of developing a single and open global standard. CCS combines single and three-phase AC charging up to 44kW as well as DC charging up to 200kW and most recently up to 350kW. DC CCS chargers are mostly available at a range of power covering 20, 44, 48 or 50kW but by 2020, 150kW, 175kW and 350kW units are becoming more available. For very high charging rates both connector and cable require liquid cooling.

Today's (2020) BEVs are capable of charging at 50kW or greater, except the e-Golf at 40kW. BEVs such as the Hyundai Ioniq at 70kW and Kona and Kia e-Niro at 77kW, and the I-Pace up to 100kW on CCS2.0. The Mercedes EQC charges at up to up to 110kW (EQC) and Audi E-Tron up to 150kW. On CCS, the Tesla Model S and X are capable of up to 140kW and the Model 3 and Y are capable of up to 150kW.

Most of today's vehicles use a 400V system voltage although some are increasing this to around 410V to 420V - both the I-Pace and E-Tron are using 450V). The CCS standard is being developed for 500A at 920V giving a charge rate of about 500kW – The Porsche Taycan is capable of a charge of up to 270kW at 850V (but only 50kW at 400V).

Tesla Supercharger Network. Meanwhile Tesla developed and rolled-out its own proprietary **supercharger** network.

Superchargers were initially available up to 90kW v1, then 145kW v2 (subsequently tweaked for 150kW) and, with v3, now up to 250kW.

The Model 3 for Europe has been configured to accept CCS and the v2 superchargers are being reconfigured to deliver both the Tesla proprietary and CCS connectors. V3 chargers in Europe will be available with CCS. Model Y and future S&X are expected to adopt the same standards.

For the v1 and v2, an eight bay Supercharger station will take grid electricity and step it down to 3-phase 480V and then feed four pairs of charger units; each unit uses twelve of the 10kW Model-S AC/DC rectifiers to deliver the high-power DC to the vehicle. Each pair of supercharger units can share power between two cars allocating the amount of power depending on each vehicle's SOC.

Tesla Model 3 at a Mode 4 Supercharger station. Photos shows a v2 supercharger outfitted for both Tesla and CCS connectors.

Photo: Karl Bown

Tesla's v3 superchargers are based around one-MW cabinets feeding 250kW to four supercharger units. V3 no longer power shares, offering full power to all vehicles connected. [102]

Tesla are also introducing the 72kW Urban supercharger – intended for urban areas, it offers a lower charge power than on-route superchargers but one better suited to a top-up charge or a destination charge. [103]

Off Street Charging

For those without off-street parking, there are solutions that can enable BEV ownership. These include lamppost charging (daytime and selected times at night), cross footpath charging, pop-up chargers, and charge bays.

Charging from a Lamp post

BEV charging from lampposts is growing in popularity[104]. Ubricity have installed more than 1,000 lamppost charge points throughout many towns and cities in the UK.[105] Lampposts typically use a single phase off a three-phase circuit and allow around 20A/4.5kW, when the light is not in use. Many authorities now turn off street lighting between 1am and 5am, or similar low use times, in low risk areas, so this should allow some night-time charging[106]. Ubricity also indicate that with some installations they can go as high as 25A/5.8kW single-phase.

Other local authorities have addressed the cross-pavement charging issue with different solutions.

Rubber cable mats can be used accepting the difficulties with pushchairs and the like. [107]

Rubber mat solution for on-road EV charging

Cut channels across the pavement/sidewalk. Users of this scheme report that provided a 'controlled parking zone' is also introduced that the solution works for them most of the time. It's a neat and simple arrangement and, for Oxford, was preferable to lamppost charging.[108]

Cross-pavement cable channel system for off-street EV charging – a very neat and practical solution in conjunction with a Controlled Parking Zone CPZ. (Photo courtesy Jesper Ekelund)

Other cities use pillar roadside chargers with restricted but fee-free parking.

Roadside EV charging

For **Apartments or Flats** there are a high number that have on-street parking and depending upon the size of the apartment block, providing charge points can be quite challenging. For Apartments with off-street parking, garage or courtyard, Landlords can be quite difficult to convince, but many are increasingly seeing the future benefit in retaining the value of their properties as more and more tenants are wanting to adopt BEVs.

However, in some cases, there is a physical constraint to the amount of electrical supply available for charging points – running feeds direct from the tenant's supply is often difficult and the power distribution company would have difficulties with so many EV chargers in one block. Using the Landlord's supply can be feasible as there is often some capacity headroom in the supply, but a power management system is necessary if the greatest number of charge points are to be provided.

A power managed power array can be used taking a three phase 100A/23kW per phase supply to provide 27 charge points at a max of 32A/7.4kW each. [109] On the basis that not all cars will require the full charge all the time, the system charges all up to the maximum of 32A until the maximum is reached when it then sheds load evenly until the minimum of 14A/3.2kW per vehicle is reached [110]. The system works well and as many Tesla owners charging regularly at 3-4kW can attest, this charge level is perfectly adequate for most users.

For new apartment blocks, planning consent should be contingent upon all spaces being provided with a power managed EV charging system. This system being much preferable to providing only a few charging points per apartment block.

Software controls charging with the fee being collected by the charge provider before being passed to the building manager – the Landlord need not be involved.

Charging times when increasing charge power

Charge Time for different battery pack sized from increasing charge power, assuming 400V system Voltage.

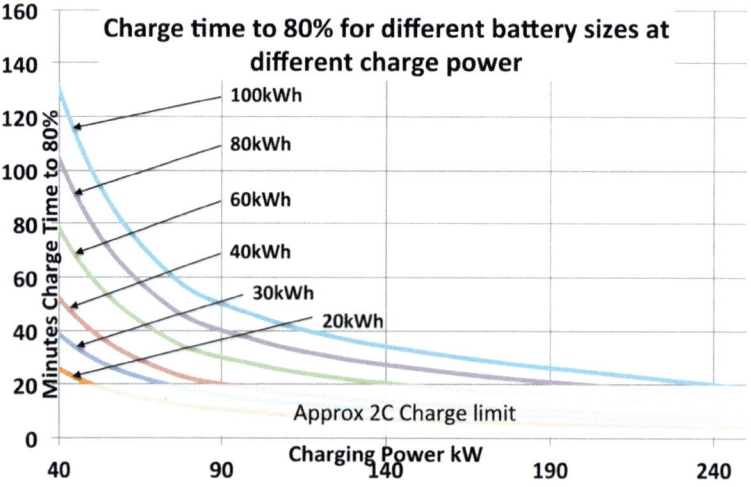

DC charging time depends upon battery size and charging power. Many of today's existing chargers are 50kW continuous (125A) into a 400V battery pack although some are restricted 44kW continuous (110A). Higher power chargers are now becoming available with a roll-out of 150kW and 250kW units. Some 350kW CCS units are also available although there are no BEVs able to charge at this power yet.

Tesla's superchargers can charge at 150kW (v2) [111] and up to 250kW (v3) [112].

Many of today's CCS chargers are 50kW continuous (125A) into a 400V battery pack although some are restricted 44kW continuous (110A). 2018/19 has seen the introduction of 150kW and, more recently, 350kW CCS units. [113]

Efficiency of Charging

The efficiency of the charging process will vary between chargers and between charging modes.

The chart below illustrates the different efficiency of a single 16A and twin 16A on-board rectifiers as well as a typical '50kw' DC charger when delivering energy into a 20kWh LMO-NMC battery pack. [114]

Clearly from this graph it is extremely inefficient to use a high-powered DC charger to deliver low power as a large proportion of the electricity taken from the grid will be dissipated as heat. This is also true of using the lower powered rectifiers at very low powers.

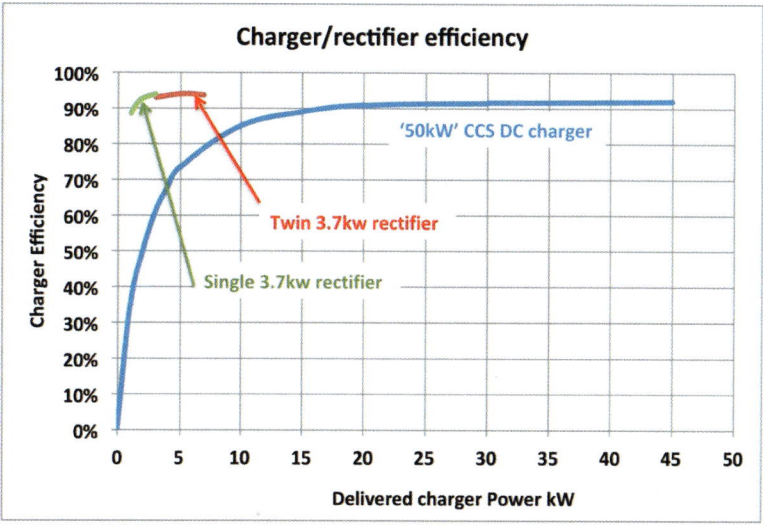

For those with battery packs of 20-40kW taking a near maximum charge is essential for mobility but as battery packs increase in size it can be expected that only the maximum efficiency portion will be taken when DC charging and one should expect a future fee structure to reflect this.

Charging rates and profiles – AC Fast and DC Rapid

Mode 3 Fast Charging

Mode 3 AC Charging depends upon the rectifier efficiency within the BEV. Depending upon the size of these rectifiers these can be around 93% but may be lower if mismatched to the charging power. Some BEVs use multiples of 3.6kW in order to match with slow, fast and three phase charging.

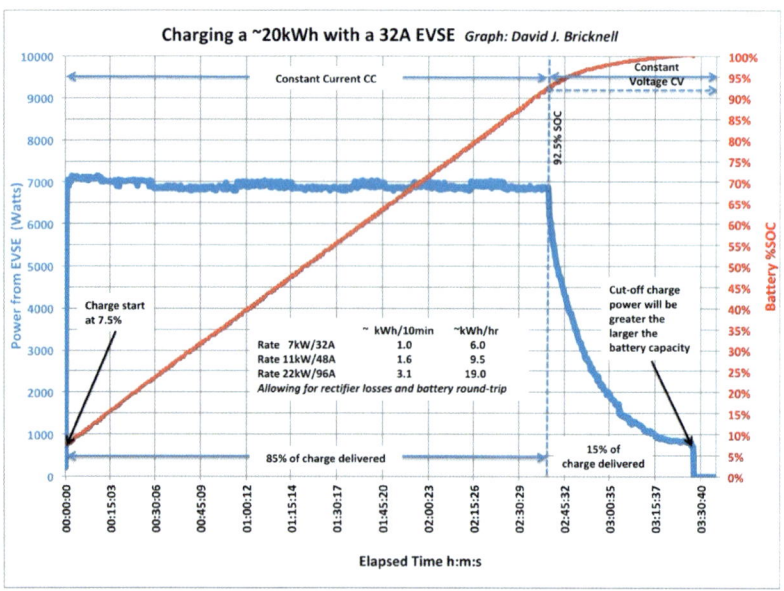

Chart showing a typical 7kW/32A/230V charge showing the distinctive CC-CV charging profile. Energy is quickly gained during the Constant Current phase and then the charge slowly completes in the Constant Voltage phase – think of it as filling a glass of Prosecco. The end cut-off charge is sharp and relates to the maximum cell voltage – the greater the capacity of the battery the higher the cut-off charge but the cut-off voltage remains the same.

Mode 4 DC Rapid Charging

Mode 4 DC rapid Charging depends on the rectifier efficiency in the off-board charging unit but typically this will be >93% (manufacturers' claim) at peak current but will reduce at lower power levels. [115]

The chart below shows the DC charging process including the reduction in charger efficiency as the battery SOC increases and the demanded power from the charger unit reduces.

Charging profiles do vary across BEVs and a multi-BEV compilation chart can be seen at the end of this chapter.

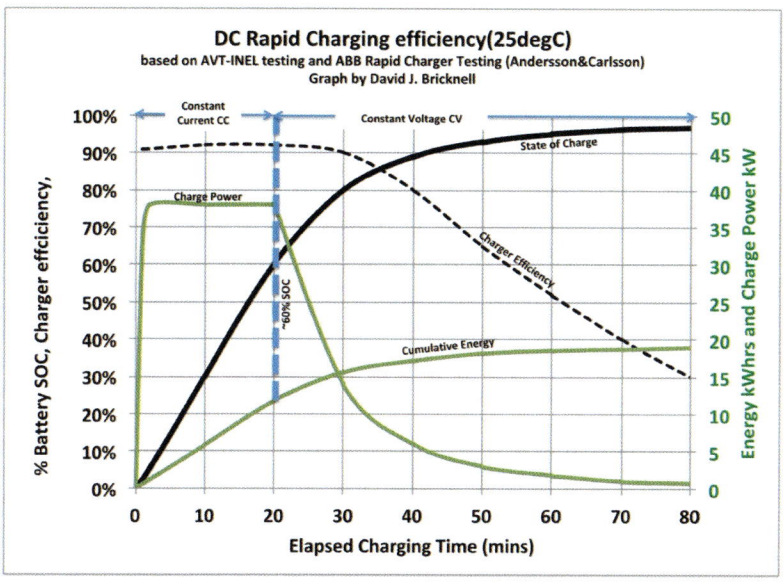

Typical CCS rapid charging of a typical 20kWh LMO-NMC battery pack at 25°C/77F

Temperature - AC Charging

When charging at AC, there are rectifier losses as well as the round-trip battery charging/discharging losses. The chart below is indicative of the losses expected through the ambient temperature range for today's BEVs.

BEVs can vary considerable with rectifier efficiency with some models being as low as 80% - some very early BEVs showed (mismatched) rectifier inefficiencies as low as 65%.

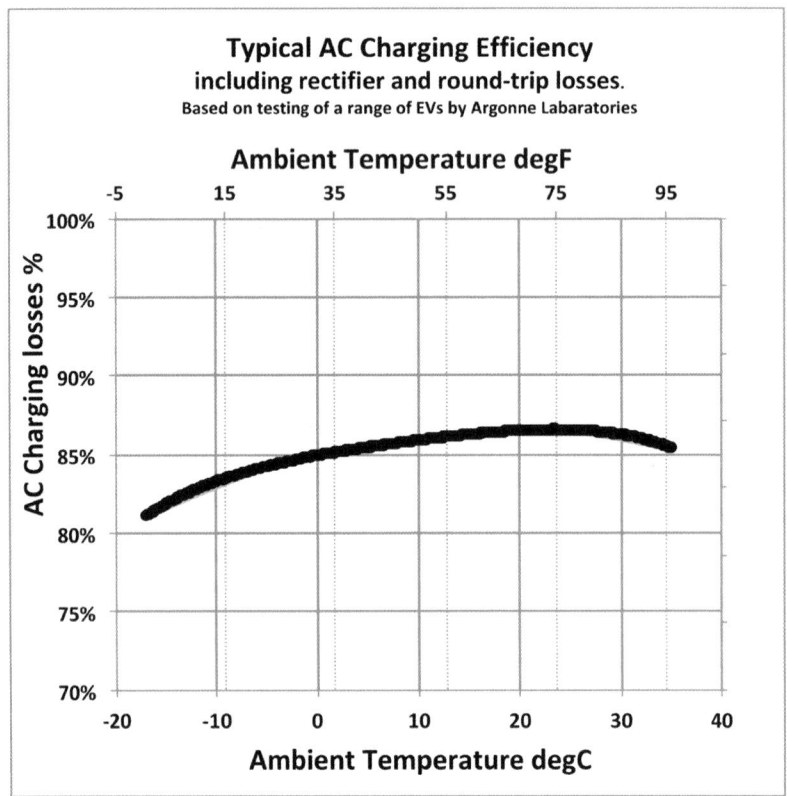

Typical 32A AC charging efficiency

- indicating losses for rectifier and for round trip battery losses.

Temperature - DC Charging

AVT-INEL conducted a series of tests on a number of BEVs including BMW i3, Nissan Leaf and VW e-Golf. This measured the rate of charge, the rate and total amount of energy taken by the battery, and the battery pack temperature rise.

Of the three ambient-temperature charging sessions, the 50°C/122°F charge was unsuccessful in the BMW i3 as the car would not enable the charge at this temperature. Li-Ion cells upper operating temperature is usually around 50-55°C. It was successful with the Nissan and VW but was very slow. Charging charts for each of these three cars is shown later in the book.

The chart below shows charging for ambient temperatures at 0°C/32°F (blue) and 25°C/77°F (red). At the lower temperature the charge is delivered at around half the power of the higher temperature the consequence of which is that the 80% charge takes around twice as long: something to be aware of when paying for time-based charging.

Overall the energy taken for the full charge is around 5% greater at the higher ambient temperature.

Battery cell temperature rose more at the lower temperature charge mostly due to the longer charge time.

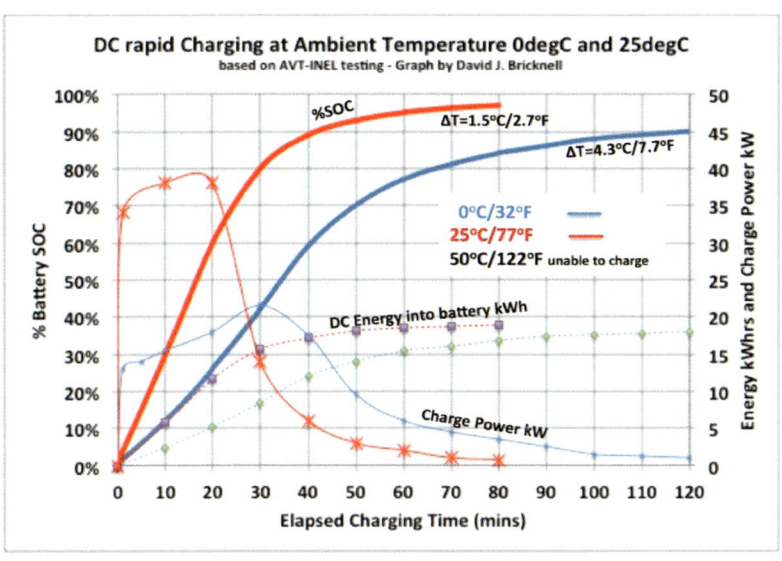

Tests on battery charging at different ambient temperatures also show a variation in charge capacity.

AVT-INEL tests showed a difference in battery capacity of about 15% between one battery pack at -6°C/21F compared to one at 35°C/95F.

The charging process itself leads to cell heating; this is true of rapid, fast and, to a lesser extent, slow charging. Hotter cells increase the ion transfer rate allowing faster charging. If cells get too hot, then the charging process can damage the cells themselves and so the BMS will either start the cooling system and/or reduce charge rate until the cells cool.

AVT-INEL has produced considerable amounts of charging information on a number of BEVs. On the Nissan Leaf with LMO Pouch Cells, air cooling and battery heating, after a 'normal' drive the following battery pack temperature rises following charging were seen:

- Rapid 50kW DC charger the average pack temperature rise at the end of charging was about 6.5°C.

- Level 2 - 7kW/240v charger showed a rise in battery pack temperature of about 2.9°C by the end of each charging session.

These rises are not significant when considered against the change in battery pack temperature changes due to ambient conditions.

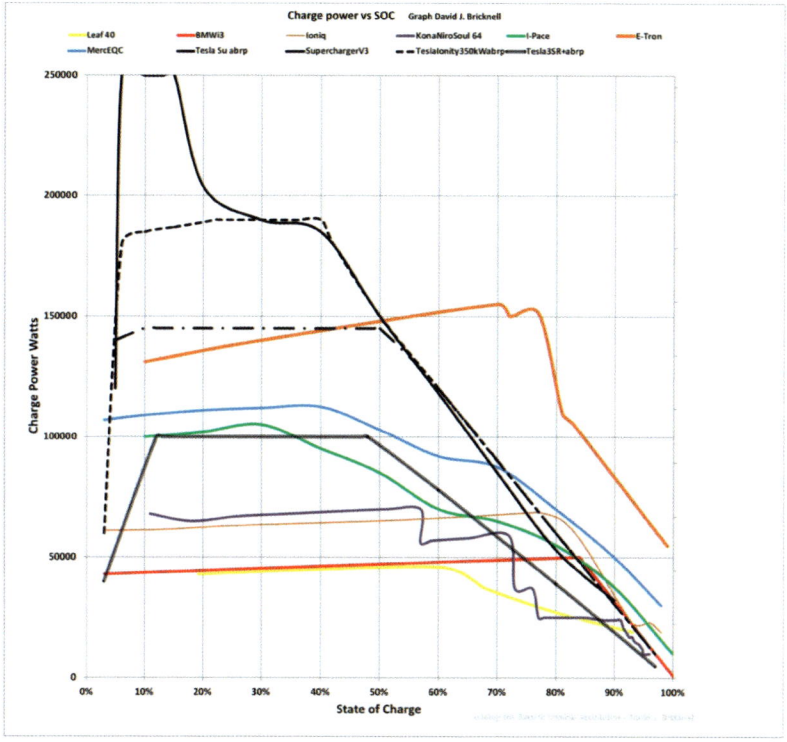

Illustrative composite DC Charging Power vs State of Charge for a number of BEVs

Common Connectors

AC

SAE J1772 is used in North America and in Japan.

Capable of 80A / 120V-240V AC / <19.2kW.

(Photo Roger Colbeck)

IEC 62196-2 or Mennekes is used in Europe on single and three-phase

Capable of 63A / 230-400V AC / <43kW (max current).

GB/T 20234.2-2011 AC is used in China

Capable of 32A / 220-400V AC / <14kW (max current)

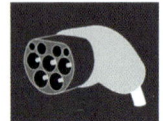

DC Only

CHAdeMO Yazaki (Nissan, Toyota, and other Japanese manufacturers.)

1.0   120A / 500V DC / <60kW (max current).

2.0. 400A / 1000V DC /160kW

3.0. 600A / 1500V DC / 500kW

GB/T 20234.3-2011 DC is used in China

Capable of 250A / 400-750V DC / <187.5kW (max current)

AC & DC Combo

SAE J1772 DC **CCS Combo** 1 used in North America and Japan

Typically, most installations are 50kW, more now available at 150kW. Latest offers 350kW.

(Photo Roger Colbeck)

EU DC **CCS Combo 2** used in Europe (BMW, Chrysler, Daimler, Ford, General Motors, Volvo, and VW Group.)

From 200V to 1000V, most installations are 50kW, more now available at 150kW. Latest offers 350kW with capability of up to 450kW [116].

Tesla – proprietary single and three-phase

V1 90kW

V2 125/145/150kW

V3 250kW

(Photo Dr Kludge CCA-2)

Tesla – CCS (Tesla implementation of CCS)

V2 150kW

V3 250kW

This page left intentionally blank

Motors, Drives and Transmissions

Overview

Battery Electric Vehicles (BEVs) are powered by electric motors with the energy coming from batteries or generators. BEVs can be front drive, rear drive or four-wheel drive; distributing electrical power can be done more flexibly electrically than with geared mechanical transmission.

Battery weight, compared to a 'tank' of fossil fuel, has been quite high so it's been important that other systems were as light and compact as possible in order to compensate for this. This situation is changing as batteries get more energy dense and electrical components become more compact, more integrated and lighter in weight.

Most motor manufacturers have taken the view that the 'drivetrain, including automotive motors are core technology and specific enough to warrant developing their own motor Intellectual Property.

Most motor manufacturers have taken the view that the 'drivetrain', including automotive motors, is core technology and specific enough to warrant developing their own motor Intellectual Property. Currently their choices differ, with a range different motor types selected for development. [117]

Earlier Tesla cars – Roadster, S and X, used Induction Machines IM either one or two, one front and one rear, for all wheel drive. [118] [119]

Renault uses a Wound Synchronous, (or Electrically Excited) Machine. [120]

GM [121], Hyundai, Kia, and Nissan [122] [123] all use Interior Permanent Magnet Synchronous Machines (IPM) whilst Jaguar uses a spoke-type IPM. All Interior PMs use an element of reluctance torque.

BMW uses a PMSyRM Permanent Magnet Synchronous Reluctance Machine (also described as an HSM Hybrid Synchronous Machine). [124]

Tesla latest models use a Switched Reluctance Permanent Magnet Machine SRPMM and a combination of SRPMM and Induction Machine in their all-wheel drive models. [125] The Model 3 was the first to use the SRPMM with the S, X and Y following.

BEV motors in use today are all DC Brushless Motors using DC current through an inverter to supply AC current to the motor. Turning the Direct Current DC electricity from the battery into AC suitable for turning the motor is the job of the Inverter. The Inverter takes DC battery power and delivers it to the motor as three-phase AC. It also acts as a converter taking AC from the motor and converting (or rectifying) it to DC to regenerate energy back into the battery.

For controlling the motor speed, most EVs use Inverters with Pulse Width Modulated Insulated-Gate Bipolar Transistors PWM IGBT: IGBTs were developed over a similar timescale to the Li-Ion battery, and their impact has been as profound as the battery in delivering efficient and usable battery powered vehicles. [126]

Tesla are the first BEV manufacturer to use SiC-MOSFETs – Silicon Carbide Metal Oxide Semiconductor Field-Effect Transistors in place of IGBTs. SiC-MOSFETs are more efficient in addition to being more tolerant of high temperatures, allowing improved range and increasing sustained speeds and accelerations. [127]

Power is transmitted to the wheels (front, rear or all) through a permanently connected, fixed-ratio gear set. In a BEV there is no need for a clutch and no need of a multiple gear set: automotive motors can provide instantaneous torque at low speeds and can extend the power through the vehicles speed range without additional gears. Gear changing would simply interrupt energy regeneration and add little useful higher speeds or faster acceleration. Motor maximum rpm for the principal BEVs range from 8000 to 20000rm.

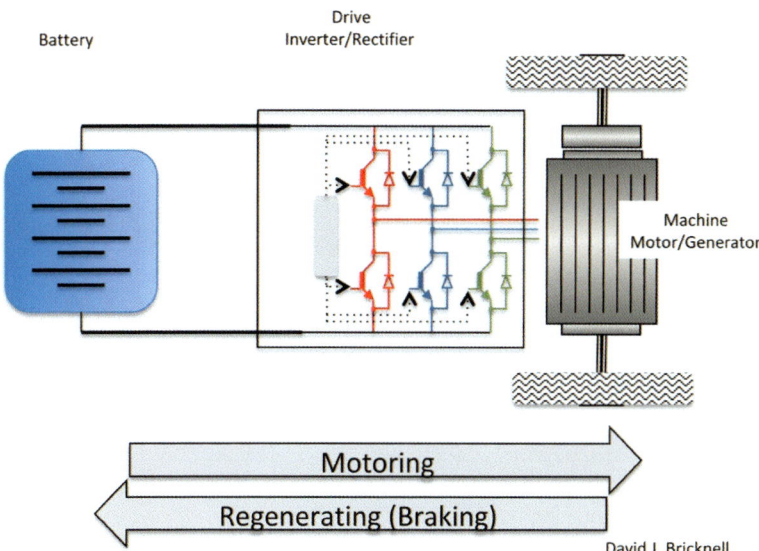

David J. Bricknell

Types of AC Electric Motors (Machines)

Motor types in use for BEVs are all AC and include both Asynchronous (Induction Machines IMs) and Synchronous Machines including Wound Rotor (or Electrically Excited) WRSM and Permanent Magnet PMSM as well as Reluctance Machines, switched or synchronous, or a combination of technologies. [128]

The term 'machine' rather than 'motor' would be the more correct one as the machine can either motor or generate - in this book both terms are used, sorry for the inconsistency.

Asynchronous 'Induction' Machine - In an AC Induction Motor IM there is a ring of electromagnets arranged around the outside (stator) and inside that is the rotor that is made up of an axle and coils of wire. The electromagnets in the stator are energized using energy from the battery so that they induce a current in the rotor thereby making the rotor rotate.

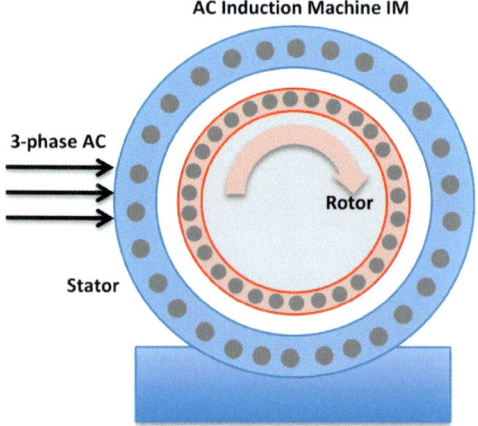

IMs are widely used and are simple, rugged and relatively low cost but are not usually as compact or as efficient as other motors. IMs don't include permanent magnets.

Tesla is the main BEV producer using IMs – until recently all Tesla's were powered by IMs. Tesla used a copper rotor cage, rather than the more usual aluminium, in order to improve motor performance although this incurs with a higher material cost [129].

Initially for the Model 3 and now for all of their vehicles, Tesla now use a Switched Reluctance Permanent Magnet Machine or, for all-wheel drive versions, a combination of SRPMM (rear) and IM (front) [130].

Synchronous Motors also have a stator providing a ring of electromagnets but instead of inducing a current in the rotor, the rotor is either wound with electromagnets excited by DC current fed from slip rings, or it has a rotor made up from permanent magnets. The synchronous motor rotates at a synchronous speed with speed control implemented by varying the supply frequency. Synchronous machines can be used as either a motor or a generator.

A **Wound Rotor Synchronous Machine** WRSM (also known as an Electrically Excited Synchronous Machine ElExSM) is used by Renault in its Zoe. WSSM are more often associated with very high-power low-speed applications exhibiting high efficiency and a high power-factor. WRSMs do not use rare-earth permanent magnets. Renault now uses an in-house designed WRSM in its Zoe having first developed a WRSM motor in collaboration with Continental. [131] [132]

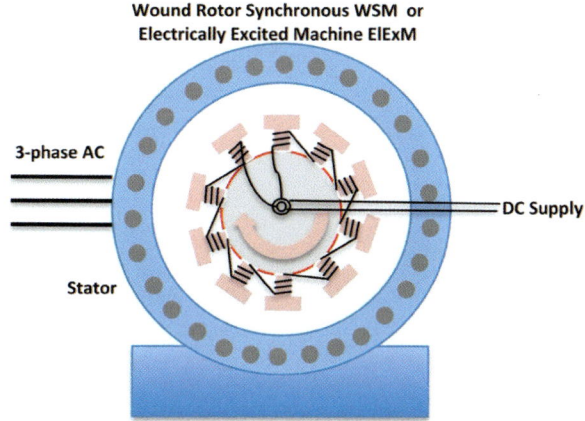

Wound Rotor Synchronous WSM or Electrically Excited Machine ElExM

Permanent Magnet Synchronous Motors PMSM use permanent magnets to provide the secondary magnetic field in the rotor eliminating the induction heat losses and providing a higher efficiency than an induction motor.

PMSMs are very power/torque dense, saving some 20% or more on motor volume and around 300W or more of winding losses [133]. Permanent Magnet Motors can be expensive when rare-earth magnets are used. Sintered Neodymium Iron Boron is the hard-magnetic material used and is a combination of Neodymium, a Light Rare Earth Element, and

Dysprosium, a Heavy Rare Earth, and which provides high temperature capability.

Rare Earth materials, despite their name, are not scares but are relatively plentiful but dispersed within in the Earth's crust. China, Australia, USA and South Africa are the major sources for Rare-Earths. [134]

Some BEV manufacturers using PMSMs use permanent magnets mounted on the surface SPM and some use them mounted internally IPM. [135] Ferrite magnets rather than rare earths can be used which can significantly reduce material costs of manufacture, but this can impact on performance. [104]

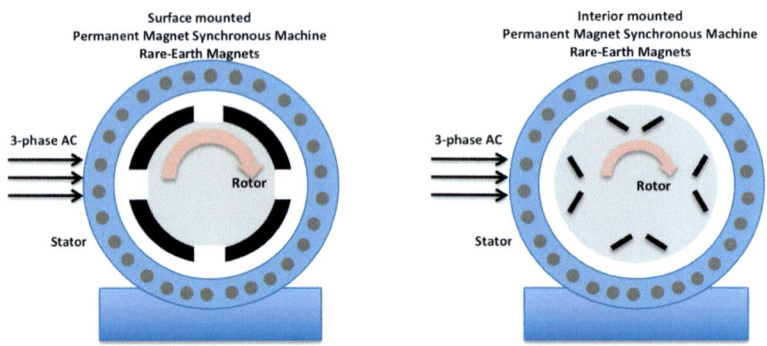

Motors can also be produced utilizing 'reluctance' torque. The 'reluctance' principle is where the rotor always tries to find its way to a position that minimizes the magnetic field energy.

A PMSM with magnets mounted in the interior, an Interior Permanent Magnet IPM, combines both reluctance torque and magnetic torque to improve efficiency whilst delivering near constant power over a much wider speed range, a high-power factor, high efficiency and a very high power-density.

The benefits of an IPM over an IM can be seen in the EPA testing when comparing EPA city cycle and highway cycle for a variety of BEVs. All the PMSM vehicle exhibit better City Cycle longer-range performance whereas IMs tend to offer longer range at Highway cycle; mostly this is attributable to improved low speed motor efficiency

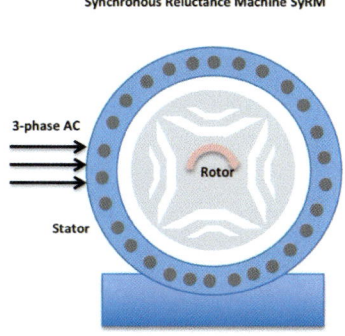

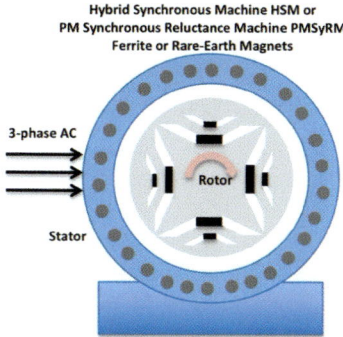

IPMs derive torque primarily from the permanent magnets but they also benefit from 'reluctance torque' derived from the shape and location of slots in the rotor laminations. They can be cheaper and smaller than SPMs because their magnets can be smaller and thinner. [136]

Adding permanent magnets, ferrite or rare-earth, to the interior of the motor produces an IPM with high reluctance torque. Both power factor and torque are improved, and the motor has good field weakening properties giving a wide operating speed range. These motors are known as Permanent Magnet Synchronous Reluctance Motors PMSyRM or Hybrid Synchronous Motors HSM.

Jaguar's I-Pace has developed a 'Spoke-Type' IPM. This configuration has allowed the use of Ferrite magnets rather than rare-earths and has produced a motor with a lower material cost whilst maintaining good performance. [137] [138]

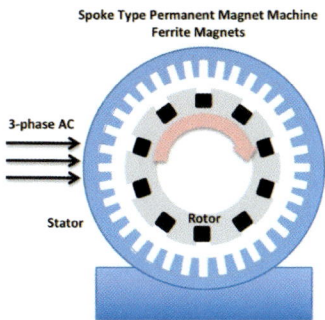

Switched Reluctance Motors SRMs are quite different from a SyRM. SRMs have a different number of stator poles to rotor poles (in order to enable self-starting) usually 8/6 or 6/4 but it can be the other way around, say 8/10, and whilst the Synchronous RM has a stator with distributed windings, the Switched RM's stator has concentrated coils. There are no windings on the rotor of either design. The Torque is produced by changing the current in the stator electromagnets and speed is controlled by modulating the torque.

Switched Reluctance Motors should be less expensive to produce, be very robust and have a very wide operating speed. Although developed as early as 1840, SRMs have been difficult to control, requiring a high accuracy of rotor position and a lot of computing power to generate the waveform that produces a smooth and responsive motor.

Adding thin pairs of Permanent Magnets to the stator poles significantly improves torque and efficiency.

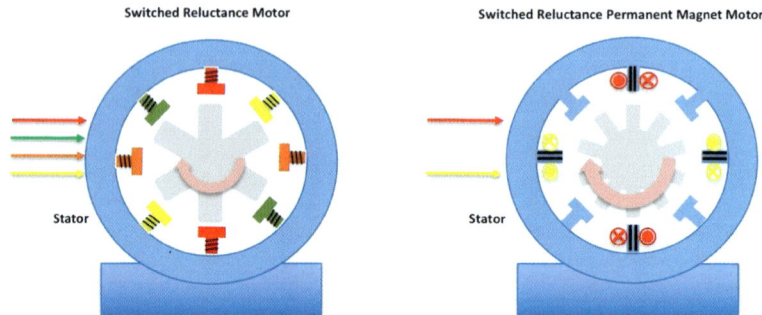

Tesla's Model 3 EPA submission states the use of 'a 3-phase AC Interior Permanent Magnet Machine using a six-pole high-frequency design with inverter controlled magnetic flux'. Elon Musk describes the motor in his tweets as 'AC induction front, switched reluctance partial permanent magnet rear'. [139]

Motor Efficiency

Each motor type exhibits its own efficiency against motor rpm and load.

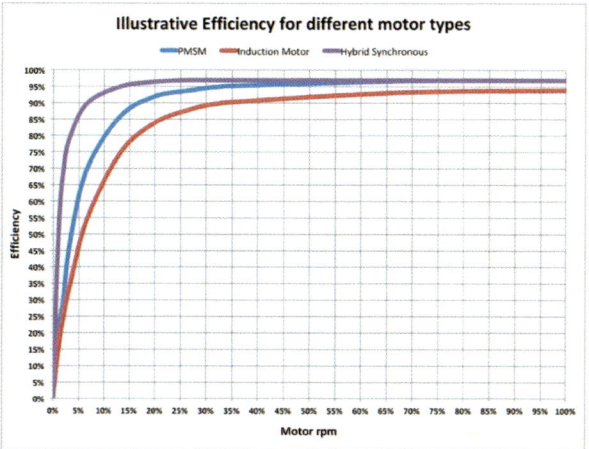

The above is illustrative of the different motor efficiency throughout the speed range.

Motor Power

The differences in power available from the different types of motors are captured in the chart below; these show motors from some of the biggest selling BEVs and shows the distinctive power curve from each type of machine.

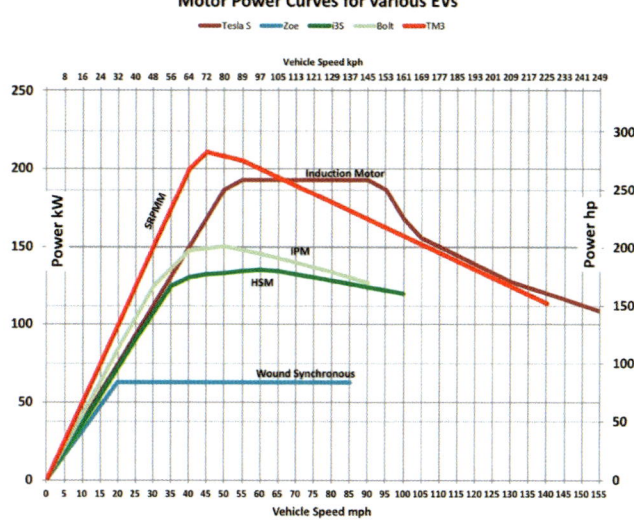

Typical power curves for a variety of motors used for Electric Vehicles.

BEV manufacturers use motors in a variety of configurations - for rear wheel drive, for front wheel drive and for all wheel drive sometimes with a single motor rear and twin motors at the front. Reducing the intrusion on the cabin space impacts on motor design – motors drive through a single-stage locked-train fixed ratio gear but some drive the shaft through a hollow rotor. GMs Bolt and the Jaguar I-Pace are using PMSMs with the driveshaft operating through the hollow rotor [140]. The Model 3 offers a highly compact drive system integrating the motor and drive electronics into one unit and driving through a single-stage, locked-train, spur gear.

Most electrical motors currently in use in BEVs are radial flux (where the flux is radial from the shaft) but considerable interest is being shown in axial flux designs (where the flux is along the shaft - think of it as a pancake style motor) because their form factor makes them very suitable for in-wheel hub drive. This technology is being adopted by buses and maybe will in the future also be adopted by trucks. Passenger cars are less likely to do so because of limited wheel diameters but these seem to be increasing in size so maybe this will also happen in the future.

Motor power will vary depending on System Voltage. As the Voltage drops, due to reducing SOC or higher C-Rate, the motor power will also drop. [141]

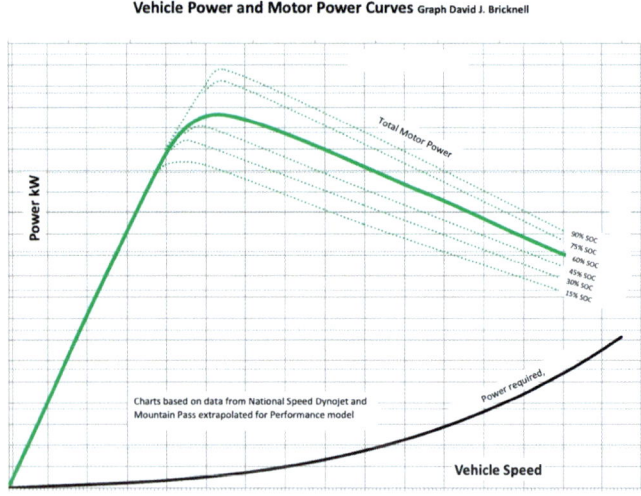

Vehicle Power and Motor Power Curves Graph David J. Bricknell

Electric Vehicles Technologies- David J. Bricknell

Power Modules

The Power Module is a Variable Speed Drive that when acting as an **Inverter** controls the electrical motor, converting the DC current from the battery into 3-phase AC and vice versa as a converter or rectifier when the motor acts as a generator. [142]

The power module is part of the electronics responsible for energy management. It takes power from the battery, (and from regeneration, and charging) and distributes power to the motor, to the resistive heating system, the refrigerant compressor, as well as the DC-DC link for powering low voltage vehicle electrical systems and for recharging of the 12V battery.

The DC-DC link reduces the voltage from the HV Battery ($\sim$ 350V depending upon battery SOC) to about 14V (similar to an ICE vehicle's alternator output) to feed the '12V' or LV system.

The power module usually contains a 3-phase 6-pack configuration of Insulated-Gate Bipolar Transistors IGBTs and emitter-controlled diodes or, as in the latest Tesla vehicles, Sic-MOSFETs (Silicon Carbide Metal Oxide Field Effect Transistors).

The power module is one key 'pinch-point' for cooling of the drive train. Power modules are usually direct liquid (water/glycol) cooled through a pin-fin type baseplate with heat then being shed through a front mounted radiator. [143]

IGBT and MOSFET modules and Inverter/Rectifiers for BEVs are manufactured by companies such as: Infineon, (including International Rectifier), Vishay Intertechnology (Siliconix), ST Microelectronics, Freescale Semiconductor, NXP Semiconductors, and Texas Instruments, and others. [144]

Insulated Gate Bipolar Transistor IGBT

Perhaps of not quite the significance to the emergence of competitive Electric Vehicles as the Lithium Ion battery but still an extremely important enabling technology, the Insulated gate Bipolar Transistor is a crucial component contributing to the efficiency of an Electric Vehicle. [145]

IGBTs are the key component in the motor drive, the DC-DC link (powering the LV components and recharging the 12V battery), the on-board charger, and the off-board rapid charger.

The IGBT was developed and introduced at a similar time to the Lithium-Ion Battery and was a key milestone in power semiconductor devices. Like LIBS, the latest generation is significantly improved over the first generation

The IGBT is a power semiconductor that has an isolated gate allowing the very rapid switching on and off of very high currents using just a small voltage applied to the gate: switching frequency is many thousands of times per second. The IGBT can be described as a voltage-controlled bipolar device. Most IGBTs incorporate an anti-parallel or Free Wheeling Diode FWD onto the chip in order to conduct reverse current: the FWD allows regeneration of energy during braking.

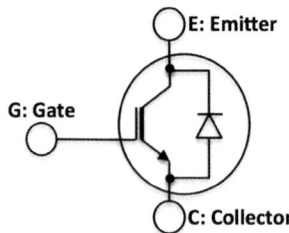

The small 'gate' voltage effectively uses the 1s and 0s of a digital controller and, because of the rapid switching frequency, the IGBT is able to produce a sine-wave from a series of digitally-initiated power pulses; this is called Pulse Width Modulation PWM, and by varying the length of the individual pulses a sine wave (or a wave-form of choice - square wave, stepped wave or a quasi-square wave) can be synthesised as the output. PWM allows smooth and efficient operation free from cogging or torque pulses.

Early motor controls used rheostats for regulating current flow through the motor but were quite inefficient: the energy not being used to drive the motor simply being dumped as heat. Thyristors, developed in the 1950s, are solid-state semiconductors capable of controlling high-power/high-voltage devices and are used extensively in inverters/speed-controllers in megawatt power installations.

Thyristors have been replaced by Power MOSFETs and by IGBTs for lower power applications: Power MOSFETs (Metal Oxide Semiconductor Field Effect Transistor) are used extensively for low-voltage motors and power supplies. The IGBT is a hybrid of the uni-polar MOSFET (which also has an isolated gate) and the Bi-polar Junction Transistor BJT, used extensively in consumer electronics such as amplifiers and radio transmitters.

IGBTs are capable of delivering up to 150kW, switching at 10kHz, and having very low losses at light loads; important for BEVs where high motor power is required for acceleration but low power for sustained 'legal' speeds.

As switching frequency increases the waveform will become smoother although because switching losses are proportional to the number of switching events then the higher switching frequencies will incur higher losses which in turn will demand higher cooling.

IGBTs are inherently forward-biased and employ anti-parallel or Free-Wheeling Diode FWD to allow for the reverse inductive current flow seen during regeneration. Regeneration occurs when the motor turns faster than the input current should drive it (known as overhauling); in that condition an inductive current will be passed back into the car and, if not dealt with, could destroy the IGBT. Regenerated power in a BEV is recuperated back into the battery.

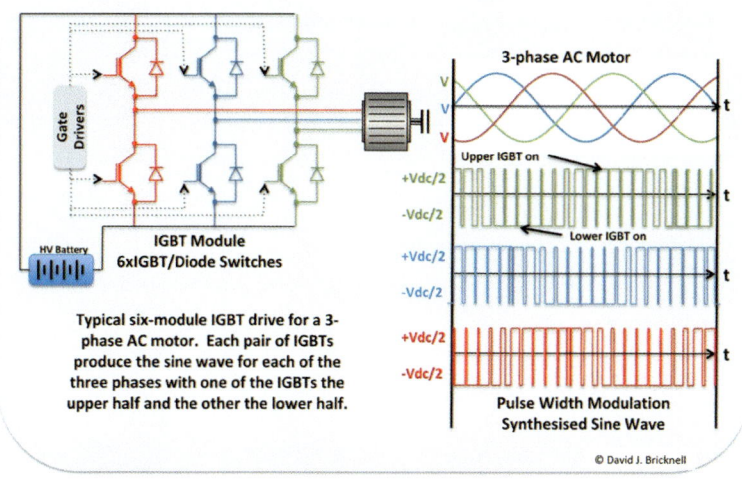

Typical six-module IGBT drive for a 3-phase AC motor. Each pair of IGBTs produce the sine wave for each of the three phases with one of the IGBTs the upper half and the other the lower half.

© David J. Bricknell

Motor drive packs are normally configured with six IGBTs or with multiples of six, i.e. 12, 18 or 24. The power module takes DC at up to 400V and produces 3-phase 360V AC for the Hybrid-Synchronous Motor. Two IGBTs per phase; one IGBT handling the upper half of the sine wave and the other handling the lower half.

There are some efficiency gains to be made from using a multi-layer inverter: instead of 6 IGBTs use 12 or 18 or 36 or more, however costs would increase significantly for a small improvement - the IGBT is a substantial proportion of the inverter cost. Tesla adopts 96 IGBTs in their drive - 16 layers of 6-pack IGBTs are connected in parallel.

For the future, if device costs are reduced, SiC-MOSFETs may replace bipolar IGBT devices in most automotive power electronics. SiC-MOSFETs have high efficiency and high power-density, exhibit high breakdown voltage, fast switching speeds and low on-resistance, as well as having a higher temperature capability. [146]

The power module inverter/rectifier motor drive is situated close to the electric motor: The power required to be delivered sets one size parameter of the pack but cooling the IGBTs to stay below the maximum junction temperature sets the physical size of the power module. The latest power packs use double sided cooling and have significantly reduced switching losses. High temperatures cause thermal stresses at the junction between the insulating substrate and the chip.

Inverters are most efficient at higher loads but exhibit good efficiency throughout the speed range.

Silicon Carbide Metal Oxide Semi-Conductor Field-Effect Transistor - SiC-MOSFET

SiC-MOSFETs have high efficiency and high power-density, exhibit high breakdown voltage, fast switching speeds and low on-resistance, as well as having a higher temperature capability. With device costs coming down and performance benefits in resisting overheating, SiC-MOSFETs have replaced IGBT devices in Tesla's models power electronics. [147]

The Tesla inverter has twenty-four power modules each containing two 650V SiC MOSFETs mounted on a pin-fin heatsink. Each power module contains two SiC MOSFETs produced by ST Microelectronics. [148]

Drive Train Efficiency

For an CEV, inefficiencies manifest themselves in combustion, in friction from moving parts and from gear and differential losses through gear meshing. Combustion losses are by far the largest but even gear losses are higher than those incurred in BEVs.

For BEVs, Drivetrain inefficiencies will include losses from battery, inverter, motor and gear.

Battery

- extracting energy from the battery causes heating of the battery cells and the higher the C-Rate the higher the losses. Similarly, the losses will increase with a colder battery cell as extracting energy becomes even less efficient.

Inverter and Motor losses

- converting DC electricity to AC within the Inverter to drive the motors - requiring cooling of the power transistors
- energy losses in the motor from rotor and stator iron and copper losses (eddy currents and hysteresis) and windage and friction losses.

Transmission losses are quite high in an ICE vehicle because of the number of gearwheels in the transmission.

Overall transmission losses will include:
- gear losses from mesh friction including lubrication losses
- bearing losses – rolling/sliding friction and lubrication losses.
- Shaft seals and unions
- Synchronization losses
- Clutch-fluid drag
- and oil pump

Typical CEV transmissions efficiencies would be [149] [150]
Manual gearbox   92-97%
Automatic Gearbox   90-95%
CVT   87-93%

For BEV transmissions most are a simple single-stage spur gear having efficiencies as high as 98-99%. [151]

Transmissions and Tyres

Electric motors provide full torque at low speeds, unlike an Internal Combustion Engine (ICE), and hence a single-speed transmission can provide the necessary performance across the vehicle operating speed range including quick and smooth acceleration from standing start.[152]

Most drivers' experience is with internal combustion engines, clutches and multi-speed transmission, whether manual or automatic. This leads many to wish for an electric motor coupled to multi-speed transmissions in order to improve efficiency and to reduce the expected noise and vibration that normally accompanies high-revving ICE. There is no need for a clutch as the electric motor doesn't turn until required and when it does it has enough torque not to stall. The motor is a rotary machine and hence inherently has a lower vibration than a reciprocating machine.

CEVs use multi speed transmission so that the engine doesn't stall under the extra loads arising from steep hills, particularly when pulling away – the classic driving test hill-start.

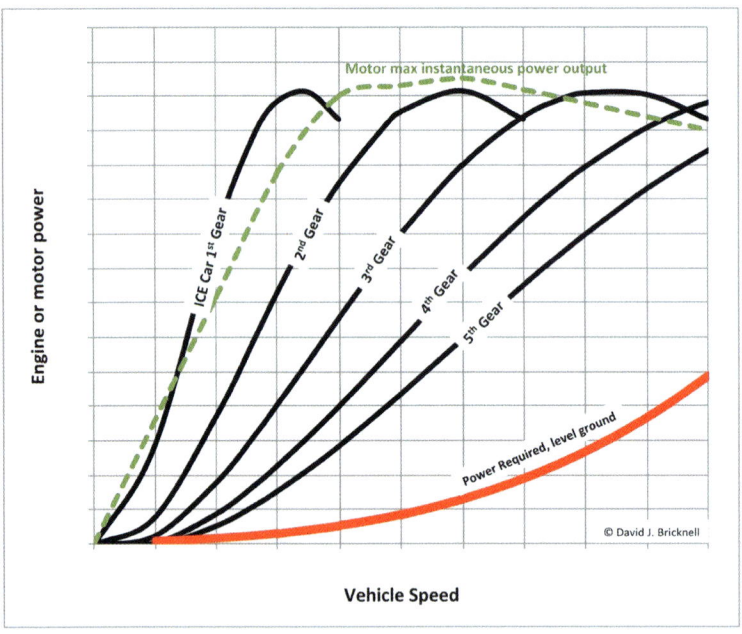

More than one transmission gear means interrupted re-generation, something that plays against energy efficiency

Across the best-selling BEVs, motor maximum rpm varies from about 8000 to 20000 depending on the motor type. Wheel sizes vary from 16" rim size to 22". Gear reduction ratio depends upon maximum motor rpm and vehicle maximum speed.

Little notice is taken of tyre size when considering a CEV. Larger, wider tyres will improve handling performance and grip however there will be a range penalty from increased weight, increased rolling resistance and poorer aerodynamics from wider tyres and less aerodynamic wheels.

Tesla state that on the S variants, changing from the 19" (245/45) to 21" (265/35) wheel/tyres will reduce range by around 3% - both tyres rolling resistance 'C'.

A similar reduction in range of 4% can be seen when changing wheel/tyres on the BMWi3 from 19" (155/70F-175/60R Rolling Resistance 'B') to 20" (155/60F-175/55R RR 'C/B') and 5% to the S with wider tyres again (155/70F - 195/50R RR 'B').

Jaguar's I-Pace, based on WLTP testing, show a 12.5% reduction in range between its highest and lowest spec versions with the lowest having 18" and the highest spec having 22" – some of this will be attributable to weight increase and some to wider and heavier wheels/tyres.

New tyres will always deliver a shorter range for the first 1000miles/1600km or so while the tyre wears in and a tyre will always produce its best range when it has the least tread depth as less energy is lost in the tread blocks. [153]

Future cars are likely to have larger diameter but narrower and more energy efficient tyres: designers prefer larger diameter wheels and the engineers prefer a narrower tyre for lower rolling resistance. Increasing a tyre diameter by 5cm/2" will lead to a reduction in rolling resistance of about 5% (or 1% per cm / 2.5% per inch), says Michelin's Damien Hallez. Contact patch is similar, so grip is maintained. [154]

This page left intentionally blank

COOLING AND HEATING INCLUDING HEAT PUMPS

Overview

Cooling and/or heating normally isn't something that would feature much when discussing CEV but for early BEVs with smaller battery packs it can have a considerable impact on vehicle range. For larger battery pack vehicles, the proportionate impact remains similar but the occasions when it becomes a concern is only for very long journeys.

BEVs use a number of different technologies for cooling of key components including active and passive air, water-glycol and refrigerants.

Cooling of an BEV's motor, drive electronics, and battery is critical to the Electric Vehicle's continuous performance.

Cabin cooling uses the same refrigerant technology as an CEV but heating, because of the lack of engine waste heat, uses either electric resistive coils or electrically driven reverse refrigerant-cycle heat pumps. Heat pumps can be around three to five times more efficient for cabin heating than resistive heating.

Waste heat from cooling drives, motors and batteries isn't currently used directly for cabin heating because of the relatively low temperatures but some manufacturers are using this waste heat to improve heat pump performance at very low temperature.

Battery cooling is required to ensure the cell temperature keeps within its operating bands; too high a cell temperature and the cell performance will be permanently damaged. Heat removed is rejected through a front-mounted radiator or, in the case of some BEVs, can be used as a heat source for the heat pump..

Where battery heat is high, the water-glycol coolant can be further cooled by running it through a refrigerant heat exchanger.

Battery heating is important in order to ensure that cell temperature is kept above a temperature that ensures it is not damaged. Cell heating is also key to performance both in energy release/acceleration and in optimising cells for rapid recharging.

Range impact

At low vehicle speeds, in very cold temperatures, the maximum energy demand for an electrical vehicle can come from the heating and ventilation system.

For a CEV it's been normal, since around the 1960s, to have a cabin heating system using waste heat from the internal combustion process; car-sized internal combustion engines have a rather poor efficiency with a significant amount of waste heat which is either rejected through the car's radiator or redirected to cabin heating, essentially for 'free'. This amount of 'free' waste heat isn't available to the more efficient electric car although some can be available from cooling the motor and electronics.

Since the 2000s, in many countries, Air Conditioning A/C has become increasingly a 'standard specification'. There is a noticeable increase in an ICE car's fuel consumption and decrease in its range (~8%-10%) when running A/C. [155]

For a BEV, range will be impacted whenever a cooling A/C demand is made. However, what comes as a surprise to many first time BEV drivers with 20-30kWhr battery packs is the magnitude of that impact on range when heating the car interior during very cold ambient outside temperatures. [156]

The graph below shows a typical reduction in range arising from the use of battery-stored energy to heat the car interior. A typical UK Summer's day will draw neither heat nor cooling but either side of that an impact is seen on range. Drivers new to BEVs often say 'there's something wrong with my battery' once winter comes but the impact is more likely coming from cabin heating.

Direct sunlight will cause a significant shift in the peak range by maybe 5 or 10°C lower in ambient temperature, such is the thermal gain from solar energy in modern vehicles glassy cockpits. In sunny climates window tinting may be beneficial, in cooler climates keep them clear.

Manufacturers of BEVs are making strenuous efforts to reduce the impact of lower ambient temperatures on vehicle range including an increasing use of more efficient heat pumps and of increased use of all sources of usable heat from electronics., motors and batteries.

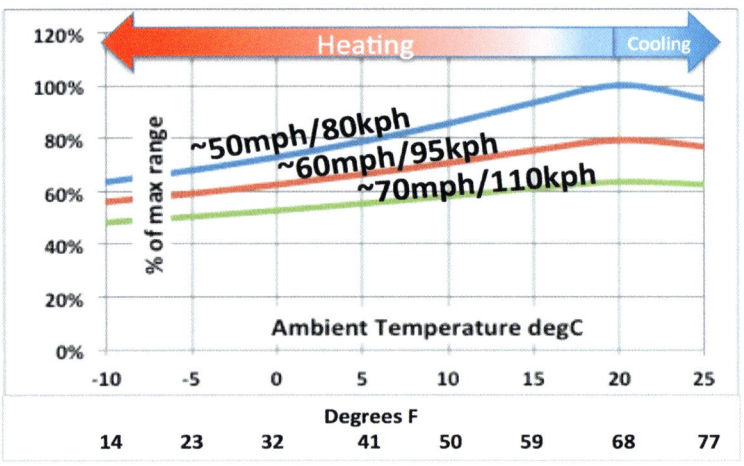

Typical range adjustment allowing for both vehicle speed and for cabin cooling and heating for Electric Vehicles.

Cabin heating varies with time and propulsion power varies with speed so the slower you go the greater the impact of cabin heating will be.

Heating and Cooling

BEVs have a number of heating and cooling systems. Given the relative simplicity of a battery and electric motor, the heating and cooling system is quite complex - BEVs need to heat and/or cool the battery and the car's interior. It also needs to cool the motor, the motor drive inverter/rectifier, and the battery charging rectifiers.

Waste heat from motors, inverters or batteries is usually not directly used to heat the passenger cabin because it tends to be too low a temperature. However, Jaguar and most recently Tesla, are using the waste heat from motor inverter cooling to improve the efficiency of the heat pump at low ambient temperatures, below zeroC and significantly below minus 10degC

Jaguar say, 'when the outside temperature is between 10°C and 15°C, the use of the heat pump rather than exclusively from the battery can extend the I-Pace range by up to 50km/30miles'. The I-Pace controls three temperatures – battery, motors and cabin; the system harvests energy from one to the other. [157]

Tesla's Model Y uses a very sophisticated heat pump system to improve efficiency by 1x to 5x compared to direct electric heating. However, by minus 10degC, heat pumps can be very inefficient, nearer 1to1, so instead of using the ambient air as the heat source, Tesla can use the power-train coolant, the battery thermal mass, the cabin thermal mass, or combinations of any of them. Such a system can also be used for battery heating and, in order to avoid a resistive heater for times when heat pump output is insufficient, the compressor can directly heat the cabin acting as an electrical heater. [158]

Battery cooling varies across BEVs – battery life will be reduced at very high temperatures and will also be reduced when the BEV is being driven hard or rapidly charged when the battery is very cold.

Some BEVs adopt passive cooling for battery temperature management some use active air cooling, some use a water glycol mix, and some use refrigerants. Battery heating, where incorporated, is usually by resistive heating although the latest Tesla's use parasitic heating arising from driving the motor with an inefficient waveform.

For cabin heating, some BEVs, notably Tesla S, X and 3, use resistive heating but increasingly more use a heat pump.

Cabin Heating

Cabin heating can be provided either by a direct resistive heater, or an indirect system using either resistive heating coils or a heat pump to heat circulating water-glycol system.

Most Tesla vehicles, except the Model Y, use direct heating. Other BEVs either use resistive heating through a water-glycol circuit or use a heat pump to heat the water-glycol circuit.

For cabin heating a number of electrical heating coils are used to provide resistive heating of a liquid that is then circulated through a heat exchanger in the cabin. For those BEVs with a heat pump, the same circulating liquid system and cabin heat exchanger is used with the heat pump output being used in place of the resistive heating circuit via another heat exchanger before it gets transferred to the cabin heat exchanger.

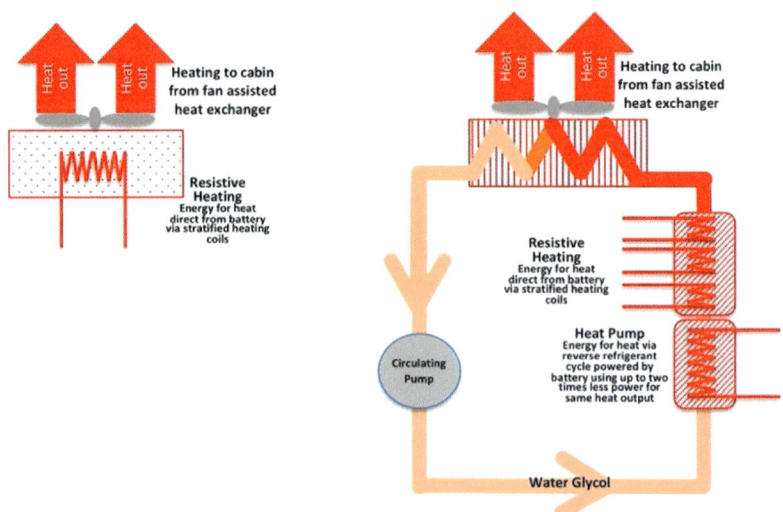

Direct and Indirect Cabin Heating systems for BEVs

Cabin cooling uses a conventional refrigerant compressor, condenser and evaporator. (See the air conditioning chart in the next section).

Heat Pumps and Refrigerant Cycle

Heat pumps, using the refrigerant cycle to deliver either cabin heat or cabin cooling, can, dependent on how low ambient temperature is, be significantly more efficient than resistive heating and its additional cost, weight and complexity can be justified when ensuring as much range is maintained in winter months. [159]

Think of the Heat Pump as a refrigerator inside out - the grille on the back of the fridge is the condenser and gets hot as the refrigerant gas becomes a liquid whereas the inside of the fridge gets cold as the refrigerant turns from a liquid to a gas. The vehicle cabin is the outside of the fridge and the inside of the fridge is now the atmosphere.

The refrigerant cycle produces heat (or cold) on about a ratio of one unit of energy to two units of heat or three units of cold by using the energy liberated when changing from liquid to gas or from gas to liquid and is hence a very efficient means of heating and or cooling. Whether heat is the objective or whether cold is purely down to positioning of the evaporator and the condenser.

Battery energy is used to drive the compressor, but ambient heat is used produce heat or cold. As the ambient temperature drops closer to the boiling point of the refrigerant, the efficiency of the system drops markedly as the amount of heat easily extracted from the atmosphere will fall.

A number of BEV manufacturers now use the waste heat from the motor and electronics to provide a higher effective ambient temperature to the heat pump thereby maintaining efficiency even to quite low ambient temperatures.

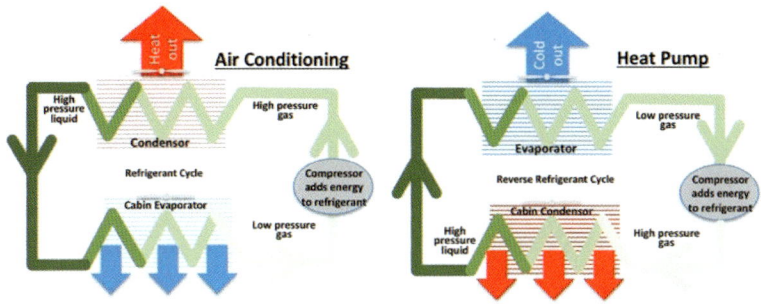

The above diagram showing the refrigerant cycle can operate in two ways – when hot, the condenser ejects heat to outside the car and delivers cold air into the car whereas when cold, the condenser is repurposed as an evaporator and ejects cold air top the outside whilst delivering hot air from the condenser into the car.

The refrigerant cycle can be from one to five times as efficient to use than a resistive heating coil dependent upon the heat source.

Using refrigerants is efficient because heat is extracted when turning the refrigerant liquid into a gas and in reverse the refrigerant gives up heat when condensing from a gas to a liquid.

The refrigerants used most often for BEVs are R-1234yf or R-134a. The normal boiling point of R1234yf is minus 29°C/-20F (R134a is minus 26°C/-15F) and, when turning the liquid refrigerant into a gas, heat will be extracted from the cabin or the battery.

R-1234yf has a Global Warming Potential GWP of just 4, whereas R134a (an HFC) has a GWP of 1440 and R-12 (a CFC, that is now no longer used) had a GWP of 8500. Some manufacturers [160] are adopting CO_2 (R-744) with a GWP of 1 but this comes with much higher pressures and a number of other engineering challenges.

When used as a heat pump the heat comes from the atmosphere (or other heat store) with the condenser being re-assigned as an evaporator. This is the same way that an air-source heat-pump uses atmospheric heat for a home installation; a ground-source heat pump uses the ground as the heat store. Some heat pumps have used a river or lake as the heat store.

As the ambient temperature gets colder, the efficiency of the heat pump reduces because the temperature differential between the atmosphere (or heat store) and the refrigerant reduces. In a BEV a 2:1 ratio for heating and a 3:1 for cooling is a useful guide.

The refrigerant system uses a:

- compressor, to add energy to the refrigerant making it a higher-pressure gas at a hotter temperature
- condenser, to turn the higher-pressure gas to a high-pressure liquid thereby releasing heat
- evaporator to 'boil' the liquid to a gas thereby extracting heat from the cabin (and battery, if refrigerant is also used for battery cooling).

In mild temperatures heat pump efficiency is high but as ambient-temperature drops the benefit of the heat pump reduces and a great amount of inefficient resistive heating will have to be used. To resolve this low temperature inefficiency, either a lower temperature refrigerant, such as CO_2, can be used, or heat can be harvested from other sources (drivetrain, battery, etc,).

Both Jaguar and Tesla have addressed this heat pump issue by using waste heat and battery thermal mass as the heat store to produce very efficient systems.

Drivetrain cooling

Whilst the BEV motor and its drive electronics (inverter/rectifier) are very efficient they are also very power-dense: waste heat removal is a key area if performance is not to be reduced. [161]

Similarly, the charging electronics with its integral AC/DC rectifier requires cooling whilst in use.

These three components use a common water-glycol cooling circuit disposing of heat through a conventional front-mounted radiator with integral electric fan – a surprise to many BEV drivers is that their car has a radiator and radiator fan.

A BEV showing the front mounted cooling radiator.
Photo courtesy of Rory Fitzgerald.

Both motor and drives are highly efficient across a broad operating range. The electric machine mostly operates between 94-97% efficiency but at lower speeds and higher acceleration loads the efficiency can drop. Similarly, whilst the IGBT or Sic-MOSFET based inverter will see high efficiencies at high motor rpms (high vehicle speeds), at lower motor rpm efficiencies will drop off.

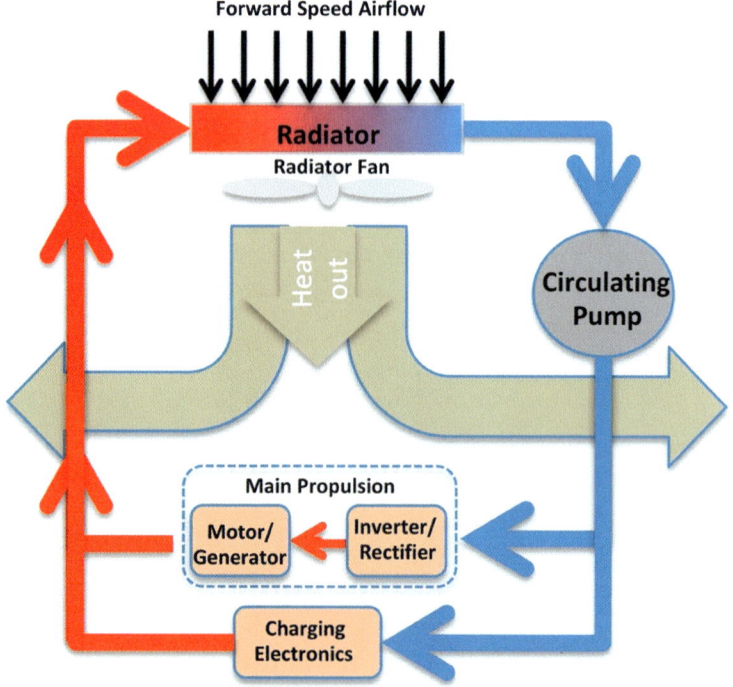

Coolant temperatures can reach 85°C/185F but unlike an Internal Combustion Engine this isn't an operating temperature to be reached in order to maximize efficiency but is something that will vary throughout the vehicle's use. There is no thermostat on this circuit and in many BEVs it isn't shared with the battery cooling system.

Where the drivetrain cooling system is integrated with the battery heating and cooling, the system gets a little more complex.

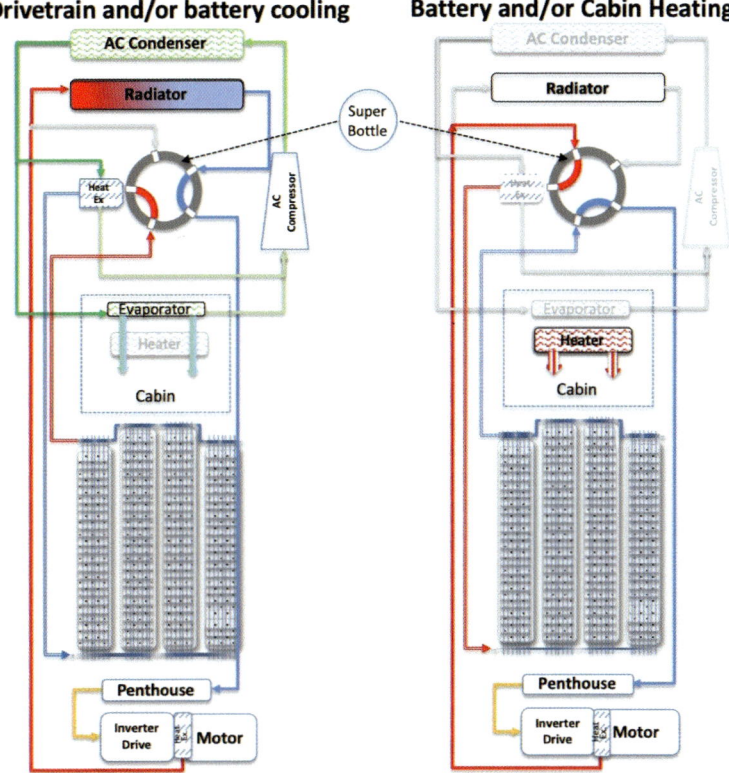

Heating and cooling system integrating the drivetrain and battery cooling and heating systems – illustrated based on Tesla Model 3.

This page left intentionally blank

Glossary

Battery – a device that delivers electrical energy from stored energy.

Battery Cell – the building block of a battery pack. Each cell contains an anode, a cathode, a separator and an electrolyte. For Li-Ion, each cell will produce a nominal 3.6 – 3.8V. Battery Cells can be 'primary' (not rechargeable) or 'secondary' (rechargeable). All BEV batteries are secondary.

Battery Module – is a collection of battery cells and is the smallest Line Replaceable Unit LRU of the battery pack.

Battery Pack – is a collection of modules with a single thermal management system. Some BEVs may have more than one pack.

Capacity – Ampere-Hour (Ah) is the nominal capacity at a specified temperature and discharge rate. For the i3 this is 60Ah and with the latest battery, 94Ah.

Capacity, rated –Watt hours or kiloWatt hours is the Ampere-Hours times the nominal voltage time the number of cells.

Current, Maximum Discharge – is the maximum current that can be delivered by the battery without sustaining damage. For the 60Ah BMW i3 this is ~ 110A. Along with the max continuous motor power this limits the car's continuous maximum speed.

Current, Max 30-sec discharge pulse current - is the maximum current that can be delivered in a 30-second pulse. For the BMW i3 this is ~ 400A and along with the motor peak power (and gearing) determines the car's maximum acceleration.

Current, recommended charge current – is the current that the vessel charges at before reaching the constant voltage phase. For the 60Ah i3 this is 110 Amps.

Battery Reversal – if a series connected set of battery cells isn't regularly balanced the weakest cell will continue to get weaker at every charge and discharge until at some point the cell will reverse its voltage causing a complete failure, often catastrophic, of the battery pack.

Battery Management System BMS – is the system, software and hardware that monitors and controls the charging and discharging of the battery and the battery temperature.

Calendar Life – is the life span of the battery under storage. It will be affected by temperature and SOC. Together with cycle-life this determines overall battery life.

C-Rate – is the battery capacity charged or discharged in one-hour.

Cathode - During Charging the ions move from Cathode to Anode. During discharge ions move from Anode to Cathode. The Cathode material is either a lithium mixed-metal oxide (typically NMC, NCA or LMO), lithium iron phosphate, or, in the case of LTO, graphite.

Cycle Life – is the number of charge and discharge cycles at a specified Depth of Discharge DOD (normally 80% of absolute SOC) that the battery can undergo before failing to meet its manufacturer's defined end-of-life. Cycle Life is affected by temperature and C-Rate. Together with Calendar Life this determines overall battery life.

Calendar Life – is the life span of the battery under storage. It will be affected by temperature and SOC. Together with cycle-life this determines overall battery life.

Depth of Discharge DOD – is the amount (%) of battery discharged compared to the maximum capacity of the battery. The higher the DOD, the lower the battery life.

Electrolyte – the electrolyte allows the ions to move from anode to cathode and back again. It is normally a liquid or gel of lithium salts and solvents. Considerable interest exists in a solid electrolyte.

Internal Resistance – varies with charging and discharging as well as under different operating conditions, such as C-Rate and temperature – hence it affects battery capacity and battery power. Increasing Internal resistance means reducing battery efficiency leading to greater battery temperature.

Lithium-Polymer – uses a microporous polymer in place of the separator. The polymer is covered by an electrolytic gel that acts as a catalyst that improves the efficiency of the ion transfer.

Power Density – is the battery peak power (kW) per battery pack unit volume (litres).

State of Charge SOC – is an estimate of the amount of usable energy remaining in the battery. Given that this will vary with rate of charge or discharge and cell temperature this is a difficult criterium to quantify accurately.

State of Health SOH – is a measure of the battery charge capacity compared to the charge capacity when the battery was new.

Specific Energy – is a measure of the capacity of the battery (Watt hours) per battery mass (kg).

Specific Power – is a measure of the battery peak power (kW) per battery pack mass (kg).

Voltage, Cut-off – is the cell voltage at 'empty' as determined by the supplier and monitored by the Battery Management System.

Voltage, Terminal – is the voltage the battery delivers under load and will reduce with reducing battery SOC.

Voltage, Nominal – is taken as the average voltage of the battery cell and is between the maximum and minimum voltage.

Voltage, Open Circuit – is the no-load cell voltage

Voltage, Charge – is the voltage that the cell is charged at. For a Li-Ion this increases during the constant-current charge phase, typically up to about 70%, and is steady at the constant-voltage phase allowing the charge current to gradually reduce until the battery is fully charged.

About the Author

About the Author

David J. Bricknell began his engineering career as an apprentice in Her Majesty's Royal Dockyard in Devonport and subsequently he studied Ship Science and Engineering at the University of Southampton.

His career in the marine world involved ship repair, shipbuilding, electronics and engineering at a number of large UK engineering companies (Vosper Thorneycroft and British Aerospace) as well as consultancy at leading UK-based global engineering company, British Maritime Technology.

At Rolls-Royce Ltd, David led the Naval design, power and propulsion sector, publishing over thirty technical papers around the world; the principles and technologies of power and propulsion being broadly similar across ships and vehicles

A responsibility for R&D as well as marine-wide business development provided the breadth of understanding across engines, transmissions as well as electrical machines, drives and energy storage.

David continues his engineering career through his own consultancy, Brycheins Ltd.

Bibliography/References

[1] "Downloadable Dynamometer Database (http://www.transportation.anl.gov/D3/) Advanced Powertrain Research Facility (APRF) at Argonne National Laboratory under the funding and guidance of the U.S. Department of Energy (DOE)". https://www.anl.gov

[2] Idaho national Laboratory - Advanced Vehicle Testing Facility https://avt.inl.gov

[3] EPA's Transportation and Air Quality Document Index System (DIS) https://iaspub.epa.gov/otaqpub/publist1.jsp

[4] MIRA (previously Motor Industry Research) https://www.horiba-mira.com

[5] National Renewable Energy Laboratory https://www.nrel.gov

[6] https://www.ornl.gov

[7] The Battery University https://batteryuniversity.com

[8] Electric Vehicles and the BMW i3 http://itunes.apple.com/us/book/id1125422107

[9] Electric Vehicles and the BMW i3 https://www.amazon.co.uk/dp/B071NW79HV

[10] http://www.amazon.co.uk/dp/1983094455 http://www.amazon.co.uk/dp/B07DH8DS54

[11] Electric Vehicles and the Jaguar I-Pace https://www.amazon.co.uk/Electric-Vehicles-Jaguar-I-Pace-Bricknell/dp/1796796360

[12] Electric Vehicles and the Tesla Model 3 https://www.amazon.co.uk/Electric-Vehicles-Tesla-Model-3-ebook/dp/B07TKN3RF7 https://www.amazon.co.uk/Electric-Vehicles-Tesla-Model-3/dp/1079466533

[13] https://www.amazon.co.uk/Electric-Vehicles-Tesla-Models-Bricknell-ebook/dp/B08GQ7K84C/

[14] Supercharged Momentum https://itunes.apple.com/gb/book/supercharged-momentum/id814894431

[15] The Tesla Roadster battery system, Tesla Motors – August 2016 Gene Berdichevsky, Kurt Kelty, JB Straubel, and Erik Toomre

[16] BloombergNEF: Lithium-Ion battery cell densities have almost tripled since 2010 https://cleantechnica.com/2020/02/19/bloombergnef-lithium-ion-battery-cell-densities-have-almost-tripled-since-2010/?source=techstories.org

[17] Net emissions reductions from electric cars and heat pumps in 59 world regions over time – Knobloch, Hanssen, Lam, Pollitt, Salas, Chewpreecha, Huijbregts, https://www.nature.com/articles/s41893-020-0488-7.epdf?

[18] Why did Porsche go to the trouble of designing an 800V Taycan EV? https://chargedevs.com/newswire/why-did-porsche-go-to-the-trouble-of-designing-an-800-v-taycan-ev/

[19] Damien Hallez, Michelin's head of technical communications.

[21] Stirling MSP calls for help to stem decline in rural petrol stations – Daily Record https://www.dailyrecord.co.uk/news/local-news/stirling-msp-calls-help-stem-

2746780

[22] CO2 Emissions from cars, the facts – A report by Transport and Environment, European Federation for Transport and Environment AISBL https://www.transportenvironment.org/sites/te/files/publications/2018_04_CO2_emissions_cars_The_facts_report_final_0_0.pdf

[23] Average UK car mileage falls again on back of higher petrol prices – The Guardian https://www.theguardian.com/money/2019/jan/14/average-uk-car-mileage-falls-again-on-back-of-higher-petrol-prices

[24] Next Move: Autobahn Test Audi e-tron against the rest of the EV world. https://nextmove.de/autobahn-test-audi-e-tron-against-the-rest-of-the-ev-world/

[25] Next Move: Autobahn Test Tesla Model X beats Audi e-Tron and Jaguar I-Pace https://nextmove.de/autobahn-test-tesla-model-x-beats-audi-e-tron-jaguar-i-pace/

[26] What Car – Real Range – Which car can go farthest in the real world. https://whatcar.com/news/what-car-real-range-which-electric-car-can-go-farthest-in-the-real-world/n18159

[27] Autocar: The electric cars with the best real world range https://www.autocar.co.uk/car-news/best-cars/electric-cars-best-real-world-range

[28] CarWOW – Electric Cars put to the ultimate range test https://www.carwow.co.uk/blog/ultimate-electric-car-range-test

[29] AutoBest: First European Independent real range test press release http://autobest.org/first-european-independent-ev-real-range-test-press-release/

[30] Tom Moloughney https://www.youtube.com/channel/UCdX0BJNon1c6GfOdeS3pyDw

[31] Electrek.Tesla Model S hypermiling record https://electrek.co/2017/06/20/tesla-model-s-hypermilling-record/

[32] Advanced Vehicle Testing Activity - Idaho National Laboratory https://avt.inl.gov

[33] Fuel Economy in Cold Weather fueleconomy.gov https://www.fueleconomy.gov/feg/coldweather.shtml

[34] Influence of Road Wetness on Tire-Pavement Rolling Resistance - Ejsmont, Sjögren, Świeczko-Żurek and Grzegorz. Journal of Civil Engineering and Architecture 9 2015

[35] "Downloadable Dynamometer Database (http://www.transportation.anl.gov/D3/) Advanced Powertrain Research Facility (APRF) at Argonne National Laboratory under the funding and guidance of the U.S. Department of Energy (DOE)"

[36] Intergovernmental Panel on Climate Change https://archive.ipcc.ch/publications_and_data/publications_and_data_reports.shtml

[37] Global warming Potentials (IPCC Second Assessment Report) https://unfccc.int/process/transparency-and-reporting/greenhouse-gas-data/greenhouse-gas-data-unfccc/global-warming-potentials).

[38] Emissions of Greenhouse Gases in the US. https://www.eia.gov/environment/emissions/ghg_report/ghg_nitrous.php

[39] Scientific American: Global Methane releases could be wetlands or wellheads https://www.scientificamerican.com/article/global-methane-releases-could-be-wetlands-or-wellheads/

[40] NASA: Global Climate Change - The Facts https://climate.nasa.gov/vital-signs/carbon-dioxide/

[41] EPA: risk assessment for Toxic Air Pollutants https://www3.epa.gov/airtoxics/3_90_024.html

[42] National Health Service NHS Air pollution 'kills 40,000 a year' in the UK, says report. https://www.nhs.uk/news/heart-and-lungs/air-pollution-kills-40000-a-year-in-the-uk-says-report/

[43] ASTM International Emissions in an Internal Combustion Engine https://www.astm.org/DIGITAL_LIBRARY/MNL/PAGES/MNL11466M.htm

[44] Particulate Matter Measurements, Burtscher and Majewski https://dieselnet.com/tech/measure_dpm.php

[45]Ultrafine particle metrics and research considerations https://www.ncbi.nlm.nih.gov/pmc/articles/PMC5129264/

[46] Study links ultra-fine particle pollution to heart disease https://dieselnet.com/news/2008/01ucla.php

[47] https://www.encyclopedie-environnement.org/en/health/airborne-particulate-health-effects/

[48] Brake, tyre and road surface wear call for evidence: summary of responses.July 2019 https://www.gov.uk/government/consultations/air-quality-brake-tyre-and-road-surface-wear-call-for-evidence/outcome/brake-tyre-and-road-surface-wear-call-for-evidence-summary-of-responses

[49] Science Direct The emissions of heavy metals and persistent organic pollutants from modern coal fired power stations https://www.sciencedirect.com/science/article/pii/S1352231007003937

[50] Net emissions reductions from electric cars and heat pumps in 59 world regions over time – Knobloch, Hanssen, Lam, Pollitt, Salas, Chewpreecha, Huijbregts, Mercure https://www.nature.com/articles/s41893-020-0488-7.epdf?

[51] Transport Energy Model – Report: Moving Britain Ahead – UK Department of Transport

[52] Tesla may soon have a battery that can last a million miles https://www.wired.com/story/tesla-may-soon-have-a-battery-that-can-last-a-million-miles/

[53] Tesla: Battery swap event https://www.tesla.com/en_GB/videos/battery-swap-event?redirect=no

[54] The Edison Nickel Iron Cell http://nickel-iron-battery.com

[55] Henney Kilowatt: The American Electric Dauphine https://group.renault.com/en/news-on-air/news/henney-kilowatt-the-american-electric-dauphine/

[56] Scotland's forgotten car: the Scamp https://www.scotsman.com/regions/glasgow-and-strathclyde/scotlands-forgotten-car-scamp-1490176

[57] The cars: Enfield 8000 https://www.aronline.co.uk/cars/enfield/8000-electric/development-story/

[58] https://www.conceptcarz.com/z19150/Chevrolet-Electrovair-II-Experimental.aspx

[59] AMC Amitron concept car from 1967 https://motor-car.net/japan/1005-amc/14101-amc-amitron-concept

[60] GM EV1 https://www.motortrend.com/news/general-motors-ev1/

[61] The Ford Ranger EV was Ford's response to the electric Chevy S-10 https://www.autotrader.com/car-news/ford-ranger-ev-was-fords-response-electric-chevy-s-10-258778

[62] The Honda EV+ Experience https://www.ecomall.com/greenshopping/hondaxx.htm

[63] Quanta Magazine Nobel awarded for Lithium Ion batteries and portable power https://www.quantamagazine.org/chemistry-nobel-goes-to-lithium-battery-innovators-20191009/

[64] Journal of the Electrochemical Society : The development and future of Lithium Ion Batteries https://iopscience.iop.org/article/10.1149/2.0251701jes

[65] Nissan Altra: A look back at the world's first Li-Ion powered EV. https://www.greencarreports.com/news/1036152_nissan-altra-a-look-back-at-the-worlds-first-li-ion-powered-ev

[66] Chemistry Department and institute for Materials Research at State University of New York.

[67] Theory of SEI Formation in rechargeable batteries: capacity fade, accelerated ageing and lifetime prediction – Matthew B. Pinson and Martin Z. Bezant

[68] Battery University https://batteryuniversity.com/learn/article/types_of_lithium_ion

[69] Insideevs: Nissan issues statement on Leaf 30kWh battery https://insideevs.com/news/337439/nissan-issues-statement-on-leaf-30-kwh-battery-degradation/

[70] TechExplore: Adding graphene girders to silicon electrodes could double he life of Lithium batteries. https://techxplore.com/news/2018-01-adding-graphene-girders-silicon-electrodes.html

[71] Tesla tweaks its battery chemistry: a closer look at silicon anode development - Christian Ruoff https://chargedevs.com/features/tesla-tweaks-its-battery-chemistry-a-closer-look-at-silicon-anode-development/

[72] PushEVS (Sept 2017) LG-Chem will introduce NCM 811 battery cells next year : https://pushevs.com/2017/09/08/lg-chem-will-introduce-ncm-811-battery-cells-evs-next-year/

[73] PushEVS (Sept 2017) LG-Chem will introduce NCM 811 battery cells next year : https://pushevs.com/2017/09/08/lg-chem-will-introduce-ncm-811-battery-cells-evs-next-year/

[74] CleanTechnica: The state of EV batteries: LG Chem, SK Innovation, & Tesla-Panasonic improvements. https://cleantechnica.com/2018/05/30/the-state-of-ev-batteries-lg-chem-sk-innovations-tesla-panasonic-improvements/

[75] PushEVS: SVOLT unveiled its new cobalt-free battery cell https://pushevs.com/2020/05/21/svolt-unveiled-its-new-cobalt-free-battery-cell/

[76] MIT Technology review Zinc-Air batteries https://www.technologyreview.com/2001/09/01/235591/zinc-air-batteries/

[77] 'World's most efficient lithium-sulphur battery' set for launch https://www.theengineer.co.uk/lithium-sulphur-battery/

[78] Lithium-air: A battery breakthrough explained https://www.theregister.co.uk/2015/11/05/lithium_air/

[79] Ceramic and polymeric.solid electrolytes for lithium-ion batteries https://www.sciencedirect.com/science/article/abs/pii/S037877531000234X

[80] BMW & Solid Power to jointly develop solid-state batteries for electric vehicles https://cleantechnica.com/2017/12/18/bmw-solid-power-jointly-develop-solid-state-batteries-electric-vehicles/

[81] Tesla completes acquisition of Maxwell, officially takes over the battery technology. https://electrek.co/2019/05/16/tesla-completes-maxwell-acquisition-battery-technology/

[82] EVTech Battery Degradation https://www.youtube.com/watch?v=XLnBg25JoHg

[83] Electric Vehicle Battery Thermal Issues and Thermal management Techniques Rugh, Pesaran, Smith NREL.

[84] certificate of Conformity-Running change to add Model S 100D and new 75kWh FW limited battery pack configuration – 80P.

[85] Argonne Electric Vehicle Testing https://www.anl.gov/es/electric-vehicle-testing

[86] InsideEVs: Tesla's tabless 4680 cell design adds energy, range and power https://insideevs.com/news/445037/tesla-tabless-cell-design-more-energy-range-power/

[87] The high voltage batteries of the BMWi3 and BMWi8 - Dipl.-Ing. Florian Schoewel, Dipl-Ing. Elmar Hockgeiger BMW Group, München https://wiki.aalto.fi/download/attachments/91692283/high_voltage_batteries_of_bmw_vehicles.pdf?version=1

[88] Insideevs: Tesla Model 3 battery cooling much improved … Track Mode? https://insideevs.com/news/338711/tesla-model-3-battery-cooling-much-improved-track-mode/

[89] Enabling Fast Charging – Technology Gap Assessment October 2017 US Dept of Energy https://www.energy.gov/sites/prod/files/2017/10/f38/XFC%20Technology%20Gap%20Assessment%20Report_FINAL_10202017.pdf

[90] Nissan's long strange trip with Leaf batteries – CleanTechnica https://cleantechnica.com/2018/09/29/nissans-long-strange-trip-with-leaf-batteries/

[91] The battery: sophisticated thermal management – Porsche Newsroom
https://newsroom.porsche.com/en/products/taycan/battery-18557.html

[92] https://www.autocar.co.uk/car-news/motor-shows-la-motor-show/new-jaguar-i-pace's-battery-electric-vehicle-technology-glance

[93] Hyundai's new battery thermal management system – Electricrevs
https://electricrevs.com/2018/12/20/exclusive-details-on-hyundais-new-battery-thermal-management-design/

[94] Android Authority:Tesla now lets you precondition your battery from your phone.
https://www.androidauthority.com/tesla-precondition-battery-825351/

[95] Battery cell balancing: what to balance and how - Yevgen Barsukov, Texas Instruments

[96] Cell balancing buys extra run time and battery life - Sihua Wen
https://www.ti.com/lit/an/slyt322/slyt322.pdf

[97] How much should you charge your Tesla overnight to keep your battery healthy and software sane – Cleantechnica https://cleantechnica.com/2018/12/07/how-to-charge-your-tesla-overnight-to-keep-your-battery-healthy/

[98] BEAMA Guide to electric vehicle infrastructure
https://www.beama.org.uk/resourceLibrary/beama-guide-to-electric-vehicle-infrastructure.html

[99] Tesla Home Charging installation. https://www.tesla.com/en_GB/support/home-charging-installation

[100] CHAdeMO releases the latest version of the protocol enabling up to 400kW.
https://www.chademo.com/chademo-releases-the-latest-version-of-the-protocol-enabling-up-to-400kw/

[101] CHAdeMO 3 released : the first publication of ChaoJi, the new plug harmonised with GB/T https://www.chademo.com/chademo-3-0-released/

[102] Tesla: Introducing V3 supercharging
https://www.tesla.com/en_GB/blog/introducing-v3-Supercharging?redirect=no

[103] Tesla: Supercharging Cities https://www.tesla.com/en_GB/blog/supercharging-cities?redirect=no

[104] Motoring Research – Electric Avenue: the first entire street with lamp post car charging https://www.motoringresearch.com/car-news/electric-avenue-lamp-post-charging/

[105] Ubricity – Intelligent residential on-street charging https://www.ubitricity.co.uk

[106] Essex – Part Night Lighting https://www.essexhighways.org/transport-and-roads/roads-and-pavements/street-lighting/part-night-lighting.aspx

[107] Hampshire County Council Electric vehicle charging – guidance for residents
https://www.hants.gov.uk/transport/ev-charging-points/ev-charging-guidance

[108] Go ultra-low Oxford – eHome Charger and Cable Gully
https://www.goultralowoxford.org/info/5/chargers/13/chargers/3

[109] Pod-Point.Array Charging https://pod-point.com/products/business/array

[110] Podpoint Array Charging https://pod-point.com/products/business/array

[111] ElectricDrive: Tesla gives European V2 superchargers 150kW
https://www.electrive.com/2019/08/29/tesla-gives-european-v2-superchargers-150-kw/

[112] ElectricDrive: Tesla puts V3 superchargers into operation in Europe.
https://www.electrive.com/2020/07/06/tesla-puts-v3-chargers-into-operation-in-europe/

[113] Motoring Research: The UK's most powerful EV charger is now open.
https://www.motoringresearch.com/car-news/first-350kw-charging-station-open/

[114] Advanced Vehicle Testing Idaho National Laboratory https://avt.inl.gov/vehicle-type/all-powertrain-architecture

[115] Measurement of ABBs Prototype Fast Charging Stationfor Electric Vehicles –
Andersson, Carlsson. Chalmers University of Technology
http://publications.lib.chalmers.se/records/fulltext/159633.pdf

[116] CharIn FAQs https://www.charinev.org/faq/

[117] Alternative Motor Technologies for Traction Drives of Hybrid and Electric Vehicles -
Dr. Sab Safi C.Eng https://assets.markallengroup.com/article-images/47910/DOWNLOAD%20THE%20FULL%20PAPER%20by%20Dr%20Sab%20Safi%20of%20SDT%20Drives.pdf

[118] Tesla Roadster – A look under the hood of the electric sports car that is generating a
buzz – kevin Bullis https://www.technologyreview.com/2008/08/19/219217/tesla-roadster-2/

[119] Induction Versus DC Brushless Motors – Wally Rippel, Tesla
https://www.tesla.com/en_GB/blog/induction-versus-dc-brushless-motors?_ga=1.71717907.161205670.1477043417&redirect=no

[120] New Zoe: The manufacturing secrets of a 100% Renault Motor. Alexandre Laurent
https://easyelectriclife.groupe.renault.com/en/expert-view/new-zoe-manufacturing-secrets-of-a-renault-motor/

[121] Design of the Chevrolet Bolt EV Propulsion System – Liu, J., Anwar, M., Chiang, P.,
Hawkins, S. et al., SAE Int. J. Alt. Power 5(1): 79-86 2016
https://saemobilus.sae.org/content/2016-01-1153/

[122] Development on an electric motor for a newly developed electric vehicle Nakada,
Ishikawa, Oki. https://www.sae.org/publications/technical-papers/content/2014-01-1879/

[123] Popular Mechanics: New Nissan Leaf motor cuts rare earth element by 40%
https://www.popularmechanics.com/cars/hybrid-electric/a8414/nissans-new-electric-motor-cuts-rare-earths-by-40-percent-14762001/

[124] The hybrid-synchronous machine of the new BMW i3 & i8 - Dr. Ing J. Merweth, BMW
Group, Munich http://hybridfordonscentrum.se/wp-content/uploads/2014/05/20140404_BMW.pdf

[125] Electrek: Tesla Model 3 dual motor performance version eatures both AC Induction
and Permanent Magnet Motor https://electrek.co/2018/05/19/tesla-model-3-dual-

motor-performance-version-ac-induction-permanent-magnet-motor/

[126] Vehicle Technologies Program – US Dept of Energy
https://www1.eere.energy.gov/vehiclesandfuels/pdfs/merit_review_2012/adv_power_electronics/ape00a_rogers_2012_o.pdf

[127] PowerElectronics: Silicon Carbibe MOSFETs challenge IGBTs.
https://www.powerelectronics.com/technologies/discrete-power-semis/article/21861356/silicon-carbide-mosfets-challenge-igbts

[128] Electric Vehicle traction motors without rare earth magnets – Widmer, Martin, Kimiabeigi https://eprint.ncl.ac.uk/file_store/production/211554/03D342FA-4EE9-4E58-A553-55632B07B13A.pdf

[129] Tesla Electric Roadster – Powered by Copper
https://www.copper.org/publications/newsletters/discover/2007/winter/pdf/dc_win2007_1.pdf

[130] Electrek: tesla motor designer explains Model 3's transition to permanent magnet motor https://electrek.co/2018/02/27/tesla-model-3-motor-designer-permanent-magnet-motor/

[131] My Renault Zoe. http://myrenaultzoe.com/index.php/2013/06/continental-press-release-powertrain-for-new-electric-renault-zoe-supplied-by-continental/

[132] Insideevs: Renault electric motor manufacture at Cleon
https://insideevs.com/news/327111/renault-electric-motor-production-at-cleon-photos-amp-videos/

[133] Science Direct.Electric Vehicle traction motors without rare earths
https://www.sciencedirect.com/science/article/pii/S2214993715000032

[134] USGS: Rare earth elements – critical resource for high technology
https://pubs.usgs.gov/fs/2002/fs087-02/fs087-02.pdf

[135] Interior Permanent Magnet Motors Power Traction Motor Applications - Kristin Green Car Reports Daily Headlines Lewotsky.
https://www.motioncontrolonline.org/content-detail.cfm/Motion-Control-Technical-Features/Interior-Permanent-Magnet-Motors-Power-Traction-Motor-Applications/content_id/789

[136] Science Direct: Basics of the electric servomotor and drive
https://www.sciencedirect.com/topics/engineering/reluctance-torque

[137] High-Performance low cost electric motor for electric vehicles using ferrite magnets – Michaelides, Mecrow, Vizan, Lisle, Martin, Goss, Gao, Long, Widmer, Kimiabeigi https://www.researchgate.net/publication/282517719_High_Performance_Low_Cost_Electric_Motor_for_Electric_Vehicles_Using_Ferrite_Magnets

[138] Autonews: Jaguar Land Rover thriving under Tata – so far.
https://www.autonews.com/article/20180528/OEM/180529809/jaguar-land-rover-thriving-under-tata-so-far

[139] Electrek: Tesla Model 3 dual motor performance version features both AC Induction and Permanent Magnet Motor https://electrek.co/2018/05/19/tesla-model-3-dual-motor-performance-version-ac-induction-permanent-magnet-motor/

[140] Autocar: New Jaguar I-Pace battery electric vehicle technology at a glance

https://www.autocar.co.uk/car-news/motor-shows-la-motor-show/new-jaguar-i-pace's-battery-electric-vehicle-technology-glance

[141] Mountain Pass Performance Tesla Model 3 SR+ Dyno Testing https://www.mountainpassperformance.com/tesla-model-3-sr-dyno-testing/

[142] The Engineering Mindset – How inverters work. https://theengineeringmindset.com/how-inverters-work/

[143] Advanced Thermal Solutions: What are the benefits of using Pin-Fin heat sinks in thermal management of electronics. https://www.qats.com/cms/2017/08/22/what-are-benefits-of-using-pin-fin-heat-sinks-in-thermal-management-of-electronics/

[144] Power Electronics Top 30 companies https://www.powerelectronics.com/community/article/21861283/top-30-companies

[145] IXYS Corporation: Insulated Gate BiPolar Transistors basics https://www.ixys.com/Documents/AppNotes/IXYS_IGBT_Basic_I.pdf

[146] IGBT or MOSFET: Choose Wisely – Blake, Bull https://www.infineon.com/dgdl/choosewisely.pdf?fileId=5546d462533600a40153574048b73edc

[147] PNT Power. About the SiC MOSFET modules in Tesla Model 3. https://www.pntpower.com/tesla-model-3-powered-by-st-microelectronics-sic-mosfets/

[148] Tesla Model 3 Inverter with SiC Power Module from STMicroelectronics – Elena Barbarini and Véronique Le Troadec http://www.oic.co.kr/files/sample_STM_SiC_Module_Tesla_Model_3_Inverter.pdf

[149] Automotive transmission efficiency measurement using a chassis dynamometer – Irimescu, Mihon, Padure https://theengineeringmindset.com/how-inverters-work/

[150] Detailed loss Modelling of Vehicle Gearboxes – Schegal, Hosl, Diel 2009. https://www.ep.liu.se/ecp/043/048/ecp09430059.pdf

[151] Gear Technology: How to minimise power losses in Transmissions , Axles and Steering Systems. – Joachim, Borner, Kurz. https://www.geartechnology.com/issues/0912x/minimize-power-losses.pdf

[152] InsideEVs.Why do Electric Vehicles only have one gear https://insideevs.com/news/334469/why-do-electric-vehicles-only-have-1-gear-video/

[153] Machine Design: Understanding rolling resistance in car tires https://www.machinedesign.com/markets/automotive/article/21831907/understanding-rolling-resistance-in-car-tires

[154] Drive: Skinny Tyres the new fashion https://www.drive.com.au/motor-news/skinny-tyres-the-new-fashion-20141004-10qelg

[155] Influence of automotive air conditioning load on fuel economy of IC engine vehicles – Kaustubh Shete IJSER Journal 2015 https://www.ijser.org/researchpaper/Influence-of-Automotive-Air-Conditioning-load-on-Fuel-Economy-of-IC-Engine-Vehicles.pdf

[156] Impact of vehicle air conditioning on fuel economy, tailpipe emissions, and electric vehicle range – Farrington, Rugh. https://www.nrel.gov/docs/fy00osti/28960.pdf

[157] https://www.jaguar.com/electrification/race-to-road/travel-further.html

[158] Tesla Model Y, EPA submission.

[159] Development of automotive air-conditioning systems by heat pump technology
https://www.mhi.co.jp/technology/review/pdf/e482/e482027.pdf

[160] RAC Daimler will phase in CO2 from next year (2015)
https://www.racplus.com/news/daimler-will-phase-in-co2-from-next-year-picture-special-15-12-2015/

[161] Progress in the development of a high performance heat sink for hybrid electric inverters – John Vetrovac
https://www.researchgate.net/publication/244653073_Progress_in_the_Development_of_a_High-Performance_Heat_Sink_for_Hybrid_Electric_Vehicle_Inverters

Printed in Great Britain
by Amazon